ZEN

ZEN STYLE

balance and simplicity for your home

with special photography by **Peter Aprahamian**

Jane Tidbury

contents

introduction

Abide in some place endlessly spacious,
clear of trees, hills, habitations.
Thence comes the end of mind pressures.

From the ancient Sanskrit text, Centering

What is Zen?

Most of us have at one time stood on a beach and been completely captivated by the sights and sounds of the sea, carried away to the point where all other thoughts seem to disappear. And perhaps, lost in the sensations of our surroundings, out of nowhere it seems, we have suddenly been struck by the beauty of a fleeting detail—a ripple of sunlight cutting through the water, the patterns of waves tumbling across the sand. We might have seen it all before, but in that briefest of moments we experience it with a new and fresh eye, as though we were seeing it for the very first time—you might say we have experienced a touch of Zen.

In the philosophical sense, a Zen teacher would probably say there is no answer to the question: What is Zen? Zen is an approach to life, a way of being, rather than a philosophy or set doctrine. It is more a personal journey of discovery which aims to free the mind so that a greater level of awareness—both of ourselves and the world around us—can be achieved. Since each journey is unique, Zen has no rules or set paths to follow. Instead, there are merely guidelines by which a person is encouraged to find and follow their own course.

Although we tend to associate Zen with the idea of deep meditation and enlightenment (both are interpretations of the meaning of the word Zen), in fact the true spirit of Zen is much more accessible.

For the central focus of Zen (the word and the teachings) concerns itself with less grandiose ideals. It is rooted in the real world and the idea that our connection with even the most ordinary of day-to-day things can provide an opportunity for insight and understanding. That even in the most mundane of tasks we can suddenly be struck by a "flash of awareness" or new way of seeing, known as Satori.

In the bigger picture, Satori is seen as the key to opening doors on the path of our Zen journey, but it is also important in its own right. Like our ripples of light in the sea, Satori is not something that can be described in words, it is something we feel intuitively without definition. But the experience of it can bring joy, a feeling of well-being, peacefulness, calm and contentment. And because of all this, it enriches us and brings a sense of balance and perspective to our lives.

The route to Satori (and possibly beyond) is through a mind that is open. If we approach the world with cluttered thoughts, preconceptions, or expectations, then we see and experience only what we expect. How do we clear our minds? Typically we might think of the dedicated monk spending hours in meditation, but that is not the only way of Zen. Even the simple act of relaxation, closing our eyes and allowing our thoughts to wander, is in itself an opening of the mind, so that when we open them again we see the world afresh.

The Zen home

If Zen is a new way of seeing, then the Zen home is about changing the way we think about our home and our relationship to it. Most of us would think of our home as a sanctuary – a place to which we retreat at the end of a hectic day. But rather than crossing the threshold to withdraw, should we not instead be crossing it to find a sense of liberation. If our home is to be a true sanctuary, then it has to be a place where we can experience new things beyond the day-to-day pressures, where we can rediscover aspects forgotten in the rush of life, and feel balanced and calm.

Zen style is not a fashion statement. Nor is it just about creating a Zen meditation space or a Japanese-inspired interior–– although, of course, it could incorporate either of these aspects. For Zen style is about self-expression—creating a space that suits each of us as an individual, allowing us to feel refreshed and enlightened when we are there.

Rather than focusing on fussy decorative treatments, the Zen approach is to think first about the fundamental aspects of the home: what we want from it; how the space can be utilized to its full potential; the relevance and position of every item we have, from the largest piece of furniture to the smallest detail.

OPPOSITE: Uncluttered outlines free the mind from distraction.

If, in clearing our mind we see more, then, in clearing our surrounding space we too can see and experience more from our home and ourselves. So the initial aim of the Zen home is to free the space of confusion and distractions and create a simplified interior. Into this we can add materials that invigorate us through color, texture and scent. For the Zen home should not become a sterile environment—a stark white minimalist setting with its own set of restrictions—but one that comes alive in the placement of natural objects, serene color and elegant shapes.

Although there is an emphasis on the application and appreciation of natural materials in the Zen home, *Zen Style* does not seek to persuade us that natural decorating is the only approach. What this book does do is invite us to go beyond the more spiritual aspects of light, space and color to seek a careful awareness of where the furniture, paints and materials that decorate the interior actually come from and how they are made. This book recommends responsible consumerism, respect for resources, re-cycling where necessary and using natural alternatives where possible to ensure that our homes are healthy places.

Whether we are able to completely rethink the place in which we live, change one room or simply adopt a shift in attitude, we can all do something to bring a touch of Zen into our homes. It begins with the consideration of a few essential elements discussed on the following pages.

Elements
of Zen

Every space can be adapted
to feel more open and calm, to
become a place where we can
find true relaxation, balance and
peace of mind. For the essence
of the Zen home is found not so
much in the choices we make
but in the thinking behind those
choices and in the essential
elements that are an integral
part of any home—the form and
structure, the light, the
furnishings and the ordinary
possessions of the everyday.

space
freedom for the spirit

We break down the confines of our home with
clean lines and streamlined simplicity to
encourage a sense of openness. In this way,
our surroundings become more fluid and
free-flowing.

light
freshness and vitality

A room flooded with daylight seems to expand the proportions of a space and diffuse the boundaries between rooms. We can relax in a room that is filled with warm light and feel instantly invigorated and energized.

natural
connecting with the spirit of life

The colors and patterns of natural objects balance the streamlined surroundings and serve to remind us of the importance and beauty of the natural world.

simplicity
uncluttering the mind and soothing the soul

A pared-down style of strong clean lines, minimal detailing and cool colors provides a setting that is without distraction.

texture

the experience of touch

A medley of different textures stimulates the senses, making the home not just a thing of beauty to be admired from a distance, but something we can feel connected to through the experience of touch.

purity

a new way of seeing

When we see something in isolation, we see it without confusion and therefore, we see it more intensely and more clearly. The color of a flower, the movement of water, the outline of an object— in their purest form, we are able to look beyond what we normally see with a fresh eye.

If our home is a retreat then it is also our escape. And the walls that cocoon us from the outside world have the potential to become our gateway to freedom.

architectural style
form and simplicity

When we think about any given room in our home, it is invariably the sense of space and atmosphere that we remember the most. Think how a room full of light with lofty, airy qualities can suddenly lift the spirit, making us feel calm as well as invigorated. And yet, in spite of this, we still tend to define a room by the objects and furnishings with which we choose to decorate it—the accessories, colors, fabrics, and the style of furniture. But often, these decorative layers mask the atmosphere, demanding our attention and directing our mind rather than releasing it. In order to create a home that is free of clutter, both actual and spiritual, we need to peel away these layers to reveal the more sensual qualities of a place. We must start with the internal structure (the division of rooms and their relation to each other) if we are to achieve a living environment that is fluid and without restriction.

To provide room for us to move and breathe, our surroundings need to be understated and without imposition. We need to feel free of our environment rather than controlled by it. A sense of space is the most important element and all other considerations should feed into this. If we were to remove the walls of our home we would have an interior landscape that is fluid and limitless. Structurally, of course, it is not practical to remove every wall, but this is, in a sense, the aim of the Zen home—to create a place that feels open, and without boundaries (or direction)—a place where we no longer feel confined by the structure.

Setting the spirit free

For the eye and mind to flow freely through the Zen home, the architectural style must be without distractions. Clean lines, pale colors, restrained repeat patterns, and smooth, uninterrupted walls and floors all help to lead the eye onwards, giving the home a sense of space. Strong shapes, outlines, and the use of symmetry bring a sense of order and balance to the architectural style. In this way, walls and floors do not jostle for attention, but recede from the eye, and the feeling of space and light intensifies.

Doorways without decorative surroundings or with the door removed, for example, frame the entrance of a room so that the eye does not dwell on the door frame but moves naturally into the room beyond. Similarly, clean outlines around a series of interior doorways seem to meld with the walls and our vision is carried onwards to the textures and colors of the next space and then the space after that.

LEFT: A system of doorways lead the eye through the house.

19

Connecting spaces

TOP RIGHT: A translucent screen provides definition for different areas of a room without dividing the space structurally.

BOTTOM RIGHT: The removal of part of a dividing wall between a small kitchen and a living area makes the kitchen seem much larger.

OPPOSITE: An internal window between two rooms links the different areas and extends the sense of space in both rooms.

BELOW: This first floor bedroom is connected visually and physically to the rest of the home by a balcony window.

Typically, our living arrangements are designed as a series of enclosed rooms which use doors to connect and close off one area from another. In certain parts of the home, such as bedrooms and bathrooms, some form of screening is necessary for privacy. However, when we take a closer look at how and why we use space generally, it would seem that for the most part, doors serve no real purpose. Even internal walls themselves can suddenly seem unnecessarily solid and inflexible. Instead of limiting ourselves to the idea of enclosed, individual rooms, we can think about how we might open up the spaces—remove whole walls or sections of wall to connect different areas. In this way, our views through the home are extended and the spaces seem to be without end. Such devices can also create a focal point, such as a long succession of rooms ending with doors that lead out onto a garden. Similarly, a setting can be enlivened by a shock of strong tone that sits in the distance of another area. Even when structural alterations are not possible, the simple step of removing a door and streamlining or widening a doorway, can bring a dramatic shift in atmosphere.

Where space needs to be divided or different areas defined, we can think about alternative and flexible options to walls and doors, such as screens that allow light through but mask the view, or sliding doors with glass or opaque panels that can close off an area when required but can also be left open to reveal the whole space. For a truly delicate division, a screen of fabric panels hung from a bamboo rail provides a subtle solution. (See page 28 for details.)

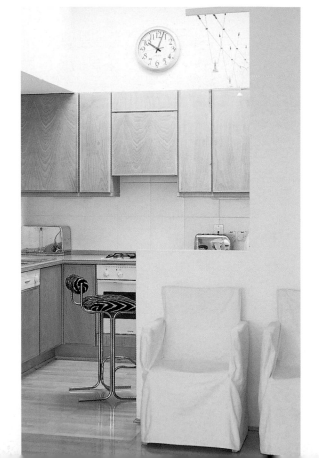

To allow natural light to flow through the home from one room to another, consider introducing internal windows. They are also an excellent device for connecting separate areas and increase the sense of space by extending the horizon. In this picture, an L-shaped figure cut into the wall between a kitchen and living room is all that is needed to link the two rooms.

THIS PAGE: The symmetry of this open plan staircase takes on an almost sculptural quality against the simplicity of the plain white wall.

OPPOSITE: Rooms are connected with sliding screens in this lofty apartment. The blue flooring provides a unifying element that also extends the sense of space.

Every exit is an entry
somewhere else.

Tom Stoppard

Walls

Large expanses of plain walls fill many people with unease to the point that there is an overwhelming desire to cover them with patterns or an array of pictures or shelves. Empty wall space is often regarded as dull and unimaginative. But in fact, a plain wall can be a beautiful thing in its own right. Effortlessly serene, its uninterrupted continuity is at once calming. It also serves to emphasize the strong clean lines of minimal architectural style.

Kept truly simple, walls can seem to disappear, making the space between them expand (although this illusion works better with pale receding colors than with deep colors.) With its rhythmic pattern and roughened suface (adding textural interest), even exposed brick work can be visually satisfying. Where decoration does remain—such as traditional plaster cornicing in old houses—it becomes an unexpected visual treat against the unadorned walls.

RIGHT: Flat painted walls set against the natural hues of the wooden doors accentuate the structure of a hallway. By keeping the design scheme simple, the clean lines take on an almost sculptural quality, increasing the suggestion of height and space, which is stunningly effective when you consider that this is just a rather ordinary hallway.

LEFT: Natural materials provide the decorative quality for these wall dividers, which give a strong, cohesive and dynamic look to a bathroom.

BOTTOM: The elegant form of a wooden hand rail becomes even more striking when set on an empty wall.

FAR RIGHT: Contrasting colors for plain, flat expanses of wall provide depth and definition in a room, and in an open-plan arrangement they can be used to signify separate areas.

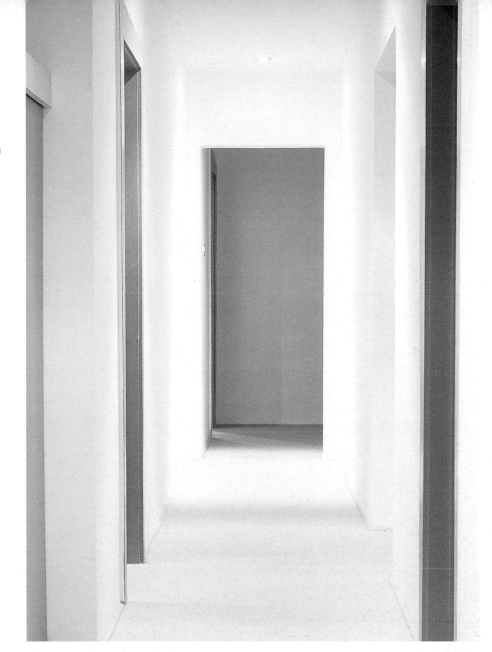

Floors

Of all the structural elements, floors—which comprise the largest single surface—have the greatest potential to influence the atmosphere in a room. By using the same treatment throughout, the floor can be used to link separate rooms, suggest continuity between spaces, and bring unity to the overall look. The most successful flooring goes almost unnoticed—it may be textured, made of natural materials, smooth or have a simple pattern—but it should always strive to be an all-over effect and never compete with other aspects of the room.

As a neutral background to a room, the quiet earthy tones of natural materials, such as wood and stone, and sisal or coir matting are ideal. Sanded floorboards are one of the simplest treatments and the easiest to maintain. Polished floorboards bring out the beauty of the grain, while "old" floorboards bring depth and character to a room. Painted boards allow you to introduce color, as do other less recognized natural products, such as linoleum and rubber. Currently enjoying a revival, these types of flooring can be bought in a wonderful range of gentle and bright colors. From a practical point of view, these floor coverings tend to be a good choice for kitchens and bathrooms, and where children are concerned, they are resilient and easy to keep clean. A calm living space can also find a perfect balance in the creamy smoothness of a painted concrete floor or the warm softness of good quality woolen carpet.

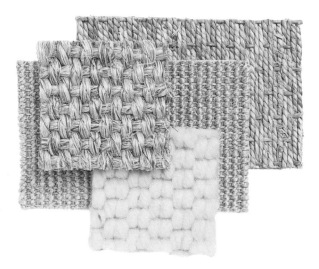

Pattern is also important. For a simple setting it should be kept regular and symmetrical—the rhythmic woven texture of natural fibers, the geometric appearance of slate or terracotta tiles—and more complex patterns should be restricted to small areas, such as rugs.

ABOVE: Wooden floorboards running from room to room provide a visual link. Use a rug to add a change in tone and texture.

LEFT: The texture of wickerwork blends beautifully with the woven pattern in a natural floor covering.

FAR LEFT: Natural woven floor coverings give a soft color to a room without imposing on the simplicity of the scheme.

OPPOSITE: Pale gray floorboards introduce a graphic quality, with the muted color accentuating the spaces in between the boards and creating the appearance of stripes.

Linen screen

Translucent panels of fabric bring definition to different areas of a room.

YOU WILL NEED:

• **150cm/60in. wide loose weave linen (or similar furnishing fabric) measuring from the floor to about 30cm/12in. below the ceiling, plus 26cm/10³/₄in. for turnings**

• **2.3m/92in. length of bamboo, 5cm/2in. in diameter**

• **2m/80in. textured rope**

• **Two large metal hooks**

• **Reel of matching cotton thread and needle**

• **Length of scrap fabric or paper**

• **Drill and drill bits**

• **Iron**

Note: if using very lightweight fabric you may need to attach curtain weights (or small coins) at the lower corners of each panel. Cut out a small oblong of the screen fabric twice as long as the curtain weight plus 2cm/ ³/₄in., and 2cm/ ³/₄in. wide. With right sides together, fold the fabric in half lengthways and stitch the side seams together to create a small pouch. Turn right side out. Slip the weight inside and turn in the open edge and hem neatly in place. Sew pockets to each bottom corner of the panel on the wrong side.

1 Working to a maximum width of 150cm/60in. decide how wide you want each of the three panels of fabric for the screen by using scrap fabric or paper taped to the bamboo pole and held in position to get an idea of the finished effect. The screen shown here used a central panel of 65cm/26in, and two side panels each 42.5cm/17in. wide. Neaten the two long sides and one short side by folding the raw edges over twice to the wrong side and machine or hand stitch in place. Press the hems flat.

2 To make a channel at the top of each panel for threading the fabric onto the bamboo pole, tidy the remaining raw edge of each panel by folding over twice to the wrong side. Pin and tack in place. Measure 11cm/4³/₈in. down from the hem and fold the fabric over to the wrong side. Pin, tack and then stitch the hem in place by working one row of stitching along the edge of the hem and one row just above it.

3 Drill a hole right through the diameter of the bamboo 10cm/4in. in from either end of the pole. Thread panels of fabric onto the bamboo support, and position in place about 20cm/8in. apart.

4 Mark the position for the screen and screw the large hooks into the ceiling corresponding with position of the holes in the bamboo pole. Using 1m/3ft. lengths at each end, thread twine through the holes in the bamboo pole and then tie securely in place to the hooks above, allowing the screen to hang about 30cm/12in. from the ceiling so that the panels of fabric sit just clear of the floor. Adjust the position of the panels on the pole if necessary.

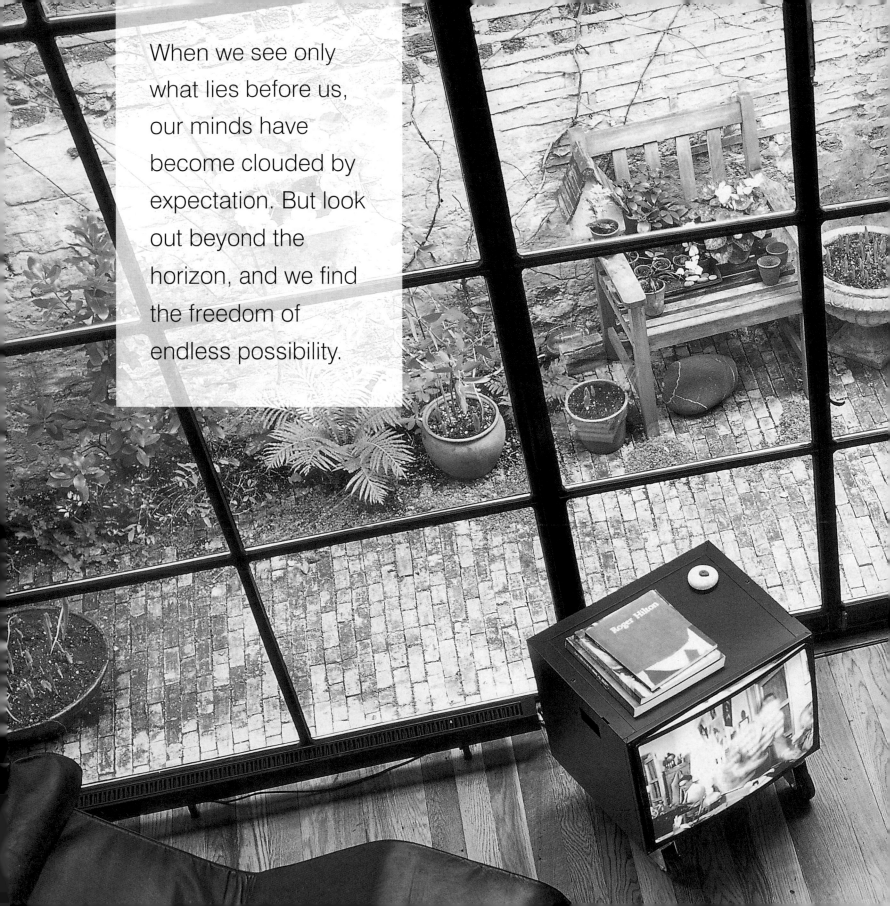

When we see only what lies before us, our minds have become clouded by expectation. But look out beyond the horizon, and we find the freedom of endless possibility.

windows
extending
horizons

One of the first things we do in the morning is go to a window and look outside. Although familiar with the view, what we see is always different: we might be surprised with the view of a bright sunny day and an endless blue sky, the dark drama of rain or even find our outlook coated with a crisp white blanket of snow. Even the subtlest changes in light can affect the colors we see and shadow shapes with new forms. The view will affect us in a myriad ways. We may feel invigorated by the seemingly infinite potential of the landscape, or protected from the force of driving rain. And as we turn back into our home these feelings remain with us.

Windows break down the boundaries of our home by leading our eyes outwards to the natural world. They increase the perception of space and suggest a greater sense of freedom. Without them, our internal space becomes oppressive and restricting. Think how differently a large open-plan area feels if there are windows at either end offering a glimpse of something more—the space seems infinitely larger and livelier than it would if our eyes suddenly came to a stop at a solid wall.

But we don't have to stand at a window to see what lies beyond. Wherever we are in our home, if a window is within our sight, so too is a view. Without realizing it, the tonal contrasts of a rooftop skyline, the treetops, and the white clouds against a blue sky are all absorbed into the ambience of our home.

Bringing the outside in

It is worthwhile considering how we can make the most of windows. They offer so much as architectural features, in their size, proportions and positioning, and in the quality of light that enters the room, which in turn will affect other design considerations such as the use of color. If windows are incorporated into the initial plans for a room, they can be exploited to the best of their potential and so improve the atmosphere of the finished area.

Most importantly windows allow us to have more intimate contact with the outdoors, and where possible, particularly in rooms that sit adjacent to the garden, we should seek to maximize this contact. A room that has the promise of a garden beyond, is revitalized by glass doors that lead straight onto a patio or deck. These doors serve to blur the boundaries between interior and exterior by allowing us to see both as we move from one to another. We can further enhance this sensation by choosing similar flooring for both areas—perhaps wooden floorboards inside leading to timber decking outside—and furniture, such as cane or wicker pieces which further emphasize the appearance of continuity.

LEFT: French doors blur the boundaries of our home—here the exterior and interior appear to be one continual space.

Letting light in

TOP RIGHT: This once dark and shadowy lobby has been revitalized with a wall of glass bricks.

BOTTOM RIGHT: An open plan setting makes the most of natural daylight flooding in from other areas of the apartment.

BELOW: A former factory has been transformed into a serene, modern home, with a roof that can be opened by remote control.

Most homes to a certain extent suffer from an uneven distribution of light. Some rooms will have a brighter aspect than others; long rooms may be dark at one end, small rooms may not have a window at all; and old houses often have an insufficient number of small windows. But the movement of light within the home does not have to be limited to external windows. There are many creative ways of increasing the amount of light flowing into certain areas.

Windows in internal walls can serve to redistribute light—bringing more light into a dark room—or connect spaces together visually, while keeping the rooms separate. To keep the look simple,

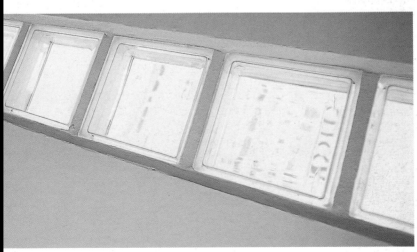

A north-facing bedroom is given a more sunny outlook with the installation of internal windows connecting the room to a large open-plan living area. Plain roller blinds provide privacy in the evenings.

RIGHT: A curtain hooked over a nail through an eyelet adds a simple decorative finish, without detracting from the straight lines of the fabric panel.

Window dressing

Window treatments can seem an unnecessary addition to the Zen home—why spoil the clean lines of the frame and obscure the view? But in many situations, we need to be able to screen our home off from the outside world, either to provide privacy, insulation, or shade from the sun on a blazing hot day.

The key question is how to retain the uncluttered theme in our surroundings while providing a practical solution for our everyday needs. Traditionally, curtains and window coverings are a decorative treatment in themselves. Unfortunately, they can sometimes be quite imposing and visually busy. The style of window dressing needs to be kept simple and streamlined so that it blends into the room without drawing our attention.

Straight panels of plain fabric that slide along a curtain pole with tabs or ties are one way of overcoming this. When drawn, the curtain will hang straight without pleats. By using a curtain pole that is wider than the window, you will be able to pull the curtain right back during the daytime to let the light flood in. Clip or peg semi-sheer fabrics onto curtain wire for a fresh, modern look. The way these fabrics filter and modify the light passing through is wonderfully evocative of the ever-changing quality of natural light outdoors.

By keeping pattern and decoration to a minimum, a simple, informal curtain will not detract from the architectural style of the window. If, however, your taste is for a little ornamentation, look for sari or voile with a delicate pattern incorporated into the fabric that will be enhanced when placed in front of the light. For a straight, flat bind, handmade papers with flecks of plant fiber diffuse the light without impinging on the airy feel of a space. Mirror the theme of strong, clean lines through a line of stitched pockets that hold single dried flowers and leaves, the use of simple decorative stripes (see pages 40-41 for details), or cottons and linens with plain checks.

Fabrics made of natural fibers are the best choice of materials, as their quality lends itself to the most casual style of curtain (see Chapter Four for a discussion of fabrics). Combined with calm colors, these fabrics will not force a visual break with the surrounding walls.

Roller blinds are another good option, as they can be rolled up during the daytime to maximize the light coming in. Wooden Venetian blinds have a symmetry that is aesthetically pleasing. Left open in a sun-drenched room, they can throw striking patterns of golden stripes across the floors and walls, or closed a little they can shield the glare—ideal for home offices. White painted shutters are a good alternative, providing clean straight lines when open and simple shapes when closed across the window at night.

BELOW LEFT: Roller blinds offer the simplest treatment for windows; conservatory blinds that unwind from the bottom upwards can be useful in situations where you want to screen your room from onlookers without blocking out the light.

ABOVE: The hues of wooden slatted blinds add warmth to a room, and their form creates mood and shadow as the light filters through.

OPPOSITE: Add a flamboyant touch to sheer pale fabrics by adding square pockets to insert natural elements of flowers and leaves.

Striped muslin curtain

Create diffused patterns of sunlight with a simple window treatment for a large or small window

YOU WILL NEED:
• **Length of white cotton muslin measuring the width of the window plus 3cm/1¹/₄in., and the length plus 4.5cm/1³/₄in.**
• **1cm/³/₈in. wide straight tape in a contrasting color (enough to run around the outside edge of the finished curtain plus 5cm/2in., plus the width of the finished curtain plus 2cm/³/₄in. by the number of horizontal stripes required)**
• **Reel of white cotton sewing thread and needle**
• **Plastic covered spring curtain wire**
• **Two small screw-in hooks**
• **Pencil or dressmaker's chalk**
• **Iron**

1 Neaten the long sides and one short side of the fabric by folding the raw edges over twice to the right side to make a double hem. (Make sure the finished hem is a little narrower than the width of the tape.) Pin, tack and stitch in place. Press the turnings flat.

2 On the right side of the fabric, mark a line 3cm/1¹/₄in. down from the remaining short raw edge. (This marks the top of the curtain.) Between this line and the bottom hem of the curtain, divide the length into horizontal stripes, approximately 30cm/12in. apart, and mark the positions. Cut strips of tape just less than the width of the curtain and place these centrally across the guide lines. Ensure that the raw edges of the strips lie halfway across the hems down the sides of the curtain. Pin and tack the tape in place and then stitch along the top and bottom edges. Press flat.

3 Cut a length of tape long enough to run around the outer edge of the curtain plus about 5cm/2in. Starting in one corner, pin and tack the tape in place around the edge of the curtain covering the outer hem and the raw edges of the horizontal stripes, and running across the guideline marked as the top of the curtain.

4 Miter the tape at the corners as you work your way around the length of fabric. When you reach the corner where you started, turn under the raw edge of tape to create a final mitered corner. Stitch tape in place by sewing along both edges of tape as before. Press flat. Fold the remaining fabric at the top of the curtain over to the wrong side using the top stripe of tape as a guide. Turn under 1cm/³/₈in. to neaten and hem stitch along the edge catching in the back of the curtain. Thread the curtain wire through this channel and fix the curtain in the window using the two small hooks.

color
in touch with the senses

Only in the palest of
settings can we experience
the true glory of color.

Color is one of the most potent elements found in nature. We see it everywhere, and are touched by the sensation of it, responding intuitively to it without thought. The luscious shade of a fabric that makes us want to reach out and touch it, the edible redness of a bowl of fresh strawberries that tantalizes our tastebuds, and the muted hues of a favorite landscape that can remind us of childhood memories. We don't just see color, we experience it.

If color is a vital part of our lives, then it is an equally important part of our home. Without color our senses are not fully alive. But what are we hoping for when we use color in the home? Do we see and experience color more acutely as a bold and daring blaze of bright yellow painted walls or do we find it in the intensity of a single yellow flower? Can the subtle shift in tone of cream and white be just as visually powerful as a sensational pattern or striking contrast? Real use of color is all about realizing its full potential, both as something to be seen and as something to be experienced. And often it is in its simplest form, uncluttered by

LEFT: The quality of different materials and surfaces brings tonal variation in this room of pure white.

other things, that we see it with most clarity.

But color is not just a thing of beauty, it is also a dynamic tool that can be used to change the sense of space in a room, emphasizing detail and providing cohesion and continuity of style. It can imbue a room with atmosphere, create a sense of calm – even affect our moods.

Most importantly, color in the home is about balance and proportion – not only in relation to the structure of the home and the atmosphere we are trying to create, but also between the different colors we use within it, whether similar shades or startling opposites. Set vibrant pink beside purple, for example, and they reduce each other to a muddy clash of tones, but set them in equal proportions against white, and they come alive with energy and vitality.

And color, of course, doesn't just come come in paint pots. We find it amongst all the things we choose to surround ourselves with, from fabrics and flooring to the natural tones of wood, saucepans, storage jars, plants and flowers, even the soap we have in our bathroom. All these

ingredients work together to make up the color schemes in which we bathe our home.

The palette for the Zen home takes inspiration from the colors found on earth, from the transient blues of seasonal skies, lakes and oceans, to the greens of moss, duck eggs and mountain pines, and the browns of soil and tree bark. Neutrals are a powerful influence, from the cereal shades of crops and honey hues of bamboo and rattan to the grays of pebbles and stones and the whites of snow, scudding clouds and the crests of a fast-running woodland stream. Into this neutral backdrop, the purity of a deep color used in isolation intensifies.

These colors find their best expression in natural dyes, which give a quiet beauty to fabrics used for soft furnishings, and as the colors fade with age, the effect only adds to the inherent beauty of the fabric. Paint manufacturers produce an incredible wealth of shades to simulate the colors of nature, but in the truest sense of Zen, we should seek our chosen colors among the available range of organic paints (see page 136).

Purity

White is, by far, the purest of colors to use in the home. Free from preconceptions, it is the color of infinite possibilities, the open arms of a room that welcome us in and encourage us to see more.

White manages to bring freshness and light to our surroundings, working well with almost any other color we may wish to introduce. It has an amazing ability to unify the setting, providing a common ground and cohesion for the most

RIGHT: In an all-white setting, the gentle changes of tone in the materials and paints become apparent, creating definition and interest.

disparate of elements. Even a traditional busy interior, for example, can be calmed and simplified with the inroduction of a shade of white.

Using white doesn't mean that a home has to become a museum, or a place that can not accommodate children. Indeed, if we are to feel relaxed at home we need to be able to live without constant worries and fears for our surroundings. Buy sofas and chairs which have removable covers, or make loose covers from quality cotton (all of which are machine washable), and apply paints on walls that can be wiped down. White, after all, is timeless; as a wall color it provides a versatile setting into which the smallest changes or additions of color can reap dramatic results. As a basic investment, it is likely to endure over the years more than any other color.

Within the single color there is a wealth of nuances of shade – the hard blueness of brilliant white, the warmer gentleness of standard white, and the many hints including chalk white, ecru, eggshell and bone, through to creams and the palest of beige. The quality of white is also changed by the material of which it is a part – the smooth sheen of white china, the textural crispness of linen, the translucence of muslin or the "patina" of an old whitewashed wall. Using these different materials in a setting can create a look that has softness as well as interest.

Combining the different shades allows you to create delicate changes of mood and depth. Build up the layers by choosing variations of shade for walls, woodwork, architraves and textiles.

Harmony

A white setting can often provide the perfect background for gentle touches of color. Used sparingly, it can be utilized to good effect, helping to highlight a particular architectural feature, exaggerate the symmetry of a room or add interest. A section of wall jutting into a white surrounding, for example, or the recesses of either side of a fireplace, become more striking when painted in a different shade from the rest of the room, and can even appear to add depth by accentuating the structural style. Plain cupboard doors, inset into a wall and painted in a complementary shade to the wall color, can be a simple way of breaking up the expanse of white without diffusing the simplicity of the architecture. Indeed, a sudden block of color heightens the impact of clean, straight lines.

Create harmony as well through the combination of colors. Balance two colors of a similar intensity, or source colors from the same tonal band to decorate a room so that there is uniformity even in variety. Similarly, use the same tonal band from one room to another to bring a cohesive force to the overall scheme.

Think about how other items might be used in juxtaposition to harmonize the elements of a space: for instance, the slate gray of a pile of stones on a white painted floor; a scattering of aubergine or muted brown cushions on a mauve sofa; the warm wheaten yellow of a willow chair in a cool white setting; even a row of glass storage jars filled with pasta and rice. These are all simple ways to harmonize different colors in a single space.

LEFT: Natural colors and textures provide warmth in a cool white setting.

BELOW: A black and white scheme for the bed works perfectly in this pared-down setting because neither color dominates.

**What is the color
of the wind?**

Zen Koan

THIS PAGE: A gradation of tones through blue and lilac bring a serene harmony of color.

TOP: A deep crimson is used to accentuate the side of the staircase and the struts of the stairwell in an otherwise white apartment.

LEFT: The clean shape of an empty fireplace is accentuated with a vivid shock of blue.

Accent

In the simplest of settings, a single note of strident color shines out the most, because we see it in isolation rather than as part of a tapestry of colors. By using accents, you can transform rooms by giving them a striking focal point.

The placement of accents of color, however, requires consideration and intent. Resist the urge to rush in with your favorite bright color: get to know your space, take a while to consider what, if anything, is needed, and always keep it simple and uncluttered. For maximum effect, keep the use of color accent to a minimum, and make sure that it works with the general color scheme.

Use a color accent for a particular element of your living space, such as your entire floor area. The bold statement will draw the rooms together visually. Use it to emphasize a feature such as a fireplace. Or try breaking with the clean lines of the architectural style with an asymmetrical jolt of color to release and refresh the spirit.

Accents can be found in the deep red and rust orange cushions that add an exotic flavor to a bedroom; splashes of vivid blue or yellow around doorways or window frames lift a plain, white hallway, and citrus colored bowls and vases in the kitchen create a warm, summery feel.

A bold vertical stripe running from floor to ceiling increases the sense of height in a room, and mirrors the sharp lines of the rectangular form. Where structural changes have been made with sections of internal walls removed to create a larger space, this device can be used to demarcate different living areas. (See pages 52-53 for details.)

It is also in the details that we find potent bursts of color: cut flowers, a single picture on the wall, or a simple rug over sanded floorboards.

ABOVE: Fresh flowers are a wonderful source of bright colors and offer a simple way to add accent to a simple color scheme.

LEFT: A white bathroom is given a buzz with accessories in lime green.

Textured stripe

A vertical stripe of mottled color provides a strong accent to pale surroundings.

YOU WILL NEED:
- **Tester pot of ivory or off-white matte emulsion**
- **Tester pot of bright blue matte emulsion**
- **Lint free cloth**
- **Wide masking tape**
- **Plumb line or spirit level**
- **Lining paper or spare paper for testing**
- **Medium-sized paintbrush**
- **Sheets of old newspaper**
- **Damp cloth**
- **Soft pencil and eraser**

Note: Before starting to paint the actual stripe onto a wall, practice the paint effect on some lining paper until you achieve a result you are happy with. Depending on the height of the wall, you may also want to adjust the width of the stripes.

1 To set the position for the blue stripe, use a plumb line or spirit level, to mark two vertical lines on the wall, 3.5cm/1³/₄in. apart, from the lower edge of the wall to the ceiling. Run masking tape down the outer edge of each line to create an outline for the stripe. Run masking tape along the ceiling and on the woodwork or floor at the base of the wall to protect these areas from paint. (Remove some of the stickiness of the tape by pressing it onto another surface before applying it to the wall. (This ensures you won't pull any paint off the wall when you peel the masking tape away).

2 Dampen your paintbrush slightly and charge with blue paint. Remove any excess paint by dabbing the brush onto a piece of newspaper. (Your brush should be quite dry so that when you draw it along the wall it leaves a mottled texture). Starting from the top, use light, downward strokes to cover the exposed area with paint. You may need to recharge your brush two or three times to complete the stripe. Work quickly and cover the whole area before the paint dries.

3 Immediately after applying the paint, wipe the stripe with a damp cloth using downward strokes. This smoothes out the texture of the paint and removes some areas of color to create a subtle, patchy finish. Work the entire length of the stripe, reworking areas lightly to achieve the finished effect. Allow the paint to dry for a few hours. Clean the paintbrush thoroughly.

4 Remove the left hand strip of masking tape. Measuring from the left-hand edge of the remaining strip, mark one vertical line 2cm/³/₄in. away and another 22cm/8⁵/₈in. away. Mask the outside area of these markers as before to create a second stripe slightly overlapping the blue one. Apply ivory paint in the same way as before. Remove all the masking tape and allow the paint to dry.

texture and materials
nature as inspiration

We are but as a pebble or a piece of wood—
of nature and part of nature.

The modern world takes us farther and farther away from our place in nature. New technology, the towering forms of cities and towns, the noise of traffic and the smell of fumes, these are the negative influences that surround us daily and push the natural world to one side. Gray, harsh, and impersonal, they overwhelm us and dampen our spirits. By contrast, think how differently we feel when we are in a natural setting; whether it's an escape to the green, open countryside or a walk along the beach, a trip to the park, or just time spent in the garden—contact with nature seems to replenish the soul.

Nature is a great leveler. Its sheer scale is breathtaking. In the presence of the awe-inspiring and the minutiae, other things rapidly become less significant—and suddenly it seems easier to decide what is important in life.

Nature is also about simple pleasures. The joy of witnessing the cycle of changes throughout the year, the excitement at seeing the first shoots of spring appear, watching them grow and blossom and then fade away to begin all over again. This

sense of continuity is written down in the patterns of nature—the rings on the bark of a tree and the ancient seams in a rock—and in seeing them, we are reminded that we are also part of the natural world and this connection provides us with a sense of belonging and a place in time. When we bring natural elements into our home, we bring all these qualities too.

We can look to the natural world to provide inspiration in our decorating style. At the same time, using natural materials to enrich our homes should not impoverish the environment. We must be careful not to squander what has taken years to grow. Choose furniture made of wood taken from sustainable forests. In some countries, products are stamped to indicate the sources of their raw materials. Where possible, look for opportunities to recycle. For example, it is now quite easy to source old wooden floorboards and furniture from salvaging companies. And perhaps, instead of buying new, scour junk shops and market stalls for pieces to use or transform.

OPPOSITE: The patterns and textures of nature embody a sense of time and continuity. We can draw inspiration from this spiritually, and as a source for ideas in the home.

Pattern and texture

The myriad patterns present in nature are ornament enough in themselves. We need to do nothing but sit back, look and enjoy—and then touch. For we can not help but want to feel the surface of a gnarled piece of driftwood, the woven structure of a cane chair or the sleek surface of smooth granite. In this way, our home becomes more than just a setting to look at, it becomes tactile as well.

If we wish to strive for a restful interior, we should create interest through the innate irregular patterns and textures of natural materials rather than the printed designs on fabrics and wallpapers that serve to distract the eye, claiming our attention. We can use these natural materials to provide a backdrop or as details and finishing touches, from sanded floorboards to a conch. Introduce objects with natural properties: metals, fabrics and earthenware; achieve textural balance by mixing the rough with the smooth, the harsh surface of volcanic stones against the cool sleek surface of a porcelain bowl. Also think about the sensation of a material—the coldness of a stone floor stimulates the feet, while the warmth of wood is more soothing.

We can also use the patterns and textures in nature as inspiration for our own creativity in the home—roughened surfaces, mottled formations, chalky substances—all of these can be interpreted as decorative effects. A layer of white on an off-white color wash applied to raw plaster (which should then be sealed with varnish), takes on a subtle patchy appearance as the plaster absorbs the color in different intensities. Used on a single expanse of wall or partition, it helps break up the flatness of pure white painted areas. Try a white plaster finish for an inherent mottled effect and simply seal with varnish. For a more dramatic look, marmorina, a plaster finish mixed with marble dust, lends a stone-like quality to a wall and can be highly polished to add luster. Similarly, a white painted wall, color-washed with ecru, takes on a hint of texture that is barely noticeable.

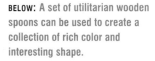

BELOW: A set of utilitarian wooden spoons can be used to create a collection of rich color and interesting shape.

RIGHT: A worn and battered piece of driftwood has a unique history, the passing of time woven into its grain and the personal memory of the moment when it was found.

OPPOSITE: A sheet of slate makes a glorious chiseled surface for a table.

To see a World in a grain of sand,
And a Heaven in a wildflower,
Hold infinity in the palm of your hand,
And eternity in an hour.

William Blake

Textiles

Fabrics provide a whole wealth of textures and their subtlety can be used effectively in the simplicity of the Zen home. In a setting that is cool, pared-back, with a concentration on clean lines and shapes, textiles used for soft furnishings inject a vital dimension of warmth and comfort—the feel of crisp cotton sheets against the skin; the luxuriance of sinking into velvet cushions; the soothing quality of diffused sunlight through an organza curtain.

The natural fibers of cotton, linen and wool are ideal for the home, as they absorb moisture and are breathable, unlike synthetic materials such as nylon and acrylic which do not. More importantly, natural fibers come from renewable resources.

Cotton is most probably the most versatile of the natural fabrics, used on all types of soft furnishings. Made from the seed fiber of the cotton plant, the yarn is woven into a tough fabric that is extremely receptive to dyes. The term covers a whole range of materials from ticking, whose light freshness is ideal for sheets and pillow cases, to softer calico for cushions, and blinds and voile for a simple sheath at the window.

Linen comes from another annual plant. The long fibers of flax are combed and spun into yarn, which is used to make linen of various weaves from coarse slub to fine matte. The finished fabric is immensely strong and hardwearing and as it ages its appearance will only improve. Linens look their best in natural, pale, or earthy colors, such as oatmeal. Hung unlined against a window, the woven pattern, with its irregularities will come to

the fore producing a gentle pattern. Lined linen offers a more dramatic, heavier look. If you feel a little more decorative detail is necessary, linen and cotton lend themselves well to drawn-thread work and simple embroidery, which do not detract from the essential character of the weave.

While cotton and linen are cool to the touch, wool is warm and springy. Fleece is prepared into wool fibres that can be woven or knitted to produce a range of textures. Choose from the regular weaving of a blanket or throw to the curly detail of wool bouclé on cushions.

Silk is the most luxurious of the natural fabrics. Made from the the tough filaments of silkworm cocoons, it comes in a variety of weights and textures. Silk has a special radiance dyed in the vivid colors of Asia. Use it sparingly in the Zen home as a color and textural accent. Hang chiffon at the window and use the nubbly surface of raw silk for a couple of elegant cushions.

Hessian is the heaviest of the fabrics, made from the fibers of the jute plant, or a mixture of jute and hemp. Used in the past for wall coverings, it is a suitable material for curtains when you want to achieve a more rugged look.

LEFT: Lush velvet cushions with an asymmetrical design create a point of interest against the woven symmetry of the wicker chair. (See pages 64-65 for details.)

OPPOSITE: Crisp white bed linen makes a stunning contrast to the honey tones of the wooden frame.

BELOW: The inherent weave in fabric is a decorative treat in itself; use a blend of different fabrics together to create softness and interest.

Velvet cushion covers

Add a touch of warmth and pattern to surroundings with sumptuous textures and rich natural hues.

YOU WILL NEED:
- **Square cushion pad measuring 40cm/16in.**
- **Brown cotton velvet measuring 52 x 42cm/21 x 17in.**
- **Cream cotton velvet measuring 52 x 42cm/21 x 17in.**
- **Reel of matching cotton thread and needle**
- **Sewing machine**
- **Measuring tape**
- **Iron**

1 Place the two pieces of velvet right sides together and sew a 1cm/³⁄₈in. seam along one short side. Press the seam open.

2 You will now have one long strip of fabric. Neaten each end by folding 2cm/³⁄₄in. under to the reverse side and fix in place with herringbone stitch. Press flat.

3 Lay the fabric on a clean flat surface with right side uppermost. From the neatened edge of the brown cotton, measure one third the length of your cushion pad, fold over and pin (wrong side now uppermost); from the neatened edge of the cream cotton measure two thirds the length of your cushion, fold over and pin in the same way (neatened edge will overlap the brown velvet by 9cm/3⁵⁄₈in.).

4 Pin, tack and machine sew along the top and bottom edges of the cushion cover across the overlap of the two pieces of material with a 1cm/³⁄₈in. seam allowance. Trim the seam turnings, press, and turn the cushion cover right side out. The overlapping neatened edges form the opening through which to insert the cushion pad.

When we see the path ahead
we no longer need to know
where we are going.

lighting

tranquility and atmosphere

Lighting is something we rarely stop and think about and yet, it affects us just as much as color and space. Light plays a major role in creating ambience in a room. We are drawn to places where the light is in harmony with our mood, from the revitalizing feel of a sunlit day to the tranquility of a room lit solely by candle-light. If the Zen home is a place where we can unwind and open our minds, then the impact of light on our surroundings is of prime importance. But the Zen home is also a place where many activities occur, and we need to make sure that we have sufficient light in order to complete them.

LEFT: Lighting can provide decorative elements to the home as well as enhancing mood and ambience.

BELOW: Simple forms meld with the surrounding design and become an elegant visual aspect as well as a practical light source.

While we may spend hours choosing furniture or deciding on the color scheme for our home, we often give very little thought to the aspect of lighting, either natural or artificial. We take the pervading mood for granted, as though it is something that is set and without possibilities.

Lighting is often chosen as an afterthought when everything else is completed or planned. But in fact, the way in which we exploit the natural daylight, and add further shape to our surroundings with artificial illumination, can have a huge impact on the finished sense of a room.

We need to consider lighting at the early stages from the point of view of how best to physically incorporate the source into a room—whether to set it out of sight or display it as a main focal point in a room. Without giving attention to lighting we miss an opportunity to make the most of a space or room, changing its rhythms whenever we want to create the appropriate atmosphere for socializing, working, reading, preparing food or watching television at the end of a long day.

The light of life

RIGHT: The sun is our greatest source of vitality.

RIGHT: The sun is our greatest source of vitality.

OPPOSITE: Large windows make the most of natural sunlight and uplift the color scheme of any room.

BELOW: Shafts of sunlight throw shadows across the wall.

Sunlight is the force of life, and just like the plants that open to its warmth, so we too become more open when we bask in its light. Over the millennia, we have adapted to the seasonal cycles of the sun, and our bodies' circadian rhythms and biological clocks are timed to perfection to follow the daily cycles of light and dark. We have also become more aware of how much we are subtly affected by light—some people are so affected by sunlight, or the lack of it, that they suffer from a condition called SAD (Seasonal Affective Disorder) which is characterized by depression, fatigue, weight gain, and a craving for carbohydrates in the dark winter months.

To be able to harness the quality of light, we must first understand it—that means getting to know a room, spending time in the space at different times of the day to see when the light is at its best, how the light flows and the colors and patterns it creates. The natural light that enters a room during the day is its focus and soul, the source from which everything else comes to life. Although this light is set by the windows, we can make efforts to highlight, shape and utilize it to the best advantage (see Chapter Two).

If the home is newly built or you have recently moved in, you might like to consider natural light when deciding how to allocate each room—a room that has the best show of light in the afternoon and early evening might be better used as a living room; whereas, a room that receives light in the morning is more suited to a bedroom or kitchen situation; and a room that has light all day long would be good for a practical space such as

an office. The changing nature of light should be taken into consideration when thinking about structural alterations. If, for example, we are opening up a space and removing walls or doorways, would it be possible to arrange the layout so that the light can shine through the entire space or rather become a focus at one end? A corner or area where there is always good light, for example, can be a prime position for a desk or reading area. A room that receives very strong sunlight for prolonged periods can sometimes have a negative impact, forcing us to shield our eyes and making us feel hot and flustered. In this instance, we need to think about ways to control the amount of light entering rather than trying to maximize its potential.

The quality of light can also influence decorative decisions. If the light is bright and golden, then additional color to a pale scheme might seem unnecessary: in a place where it is cool, use of color might be a better option to add a sense of depth and spirit to an area. And in a place where glorious splashes of light are formed across the walls and floors, other elements may be kept to a minimum and lines and details kept pure to allow the light patterns to become the focus.

Light as practical

Although natural sunlight is the preferred choice for illuminating the home, artificial lighting is often the only option we have, especially in colder climates or during the winter months. But artificial lighting can still have a remarkable effect in the Zen home when used correctly. And indeed, if we are to find more pleasure in everyday tasks, then good lighting, which can also make a job easier, is just as important as aesthetic considerations. Practical lighting needs to be discreetly set so as not to confuse or clutter the streamlined view. Practical lighting comes in the form of ambient and task lighting.

The former of these creates the general ambience of a room. It should be flexible so that it can be altered to suit lighting needs throughout the day, but so well designed that we barely notice it. In large areas it becomes the understudy for natural daylight; in smaller, more enclosed situations, it illuminates our way without fuss. Task lighting directs light into a particular discrete area, such as over a desk, or beside a bed for reading. In most rooms, try using a variety of light

RIGHT: Recessed lighting in the ceiling of this kitchen illustrate well thought out illumination for practical tasks without detracting from the style and simplicity of the room.

sources—downlights, spotlights, tungsten-halo-gen uplighters, and desk lights to achieve a flexible lighting scheme that covers all the activities that will go on in that room. Try to avoid fluorescent lights as they can make you tired and irritable—if you have to use them at all, try and replace the tube for a natural-daylight one.

Assess how each room is used, and where different tasks are performed. In a kitchen, a lighting system in the ceiling with the option to "direct" the light to different areas, works well—if attached to a dimmer switch a softer mood can be created in the evening, especially useful where there is an dining area within the same room. If wall cupboards are set over work surfaces, lighting can be tucked underneath to throw light down into the shadowy area below and directly onto the place where food is being prepared. A hallway requires a continuous distribution of light flowing through the space—again, recessed ceiling lights can be discreet and effective, but make sure there are enough placed at regular intervals to create one whole sense of light rather than a series of pools.

Although a living area requires mood and coziness at night, a backdrop of uniform lighting is equally important for darker days and times when we want good, clean illumination. Again, we want to create a continuous spread of light that lifts the room rather than filling it with shadows. Consider setting these lights in groups connected to a series of switches—in this way we have the option for lowering the level of light or just illuminating one selected area, and this can be useful for creating a more relaxed atmosphere in the evening.

The style of light is an important consideration. Recessed lights that can be fitted flush with the

LEFT: Downlighters provide a directional light for bedtime reading.

ceiling are one of the most low-key options. The angle of light can be directed, just as with conventional spots, but the appearance is more sleek and less imposing than fittings which hang from the ceiling. Fine halogen lights set on a taut wire running across a room, also have a simple appearance—the straight lines of the cable serve to reflect the lines of the architectural structure. In a functional room, such as a kitchen, the simple outline of spotlights can work well as a foil to the utilitarian aspect of the fittings. Opt for clean, simple shapes in white or chrome rather than convoluted designs in bright colors. Anglepoise lamps, which are excellent for providing directed light over a desk area, have undergone something of a style transformation and can be a sleek addition to a room while still being practical. Choose slim, streamlined looks that retain a sense of simplicity.

The moment we are enlightened within, we go beyond the voidness of a world confronting us.

Zen Haiku

RIGHT AND BELOW: Look for striking clear shapes for lamps that can become a decorative focus in a room as well as supplying a diffused source of light.

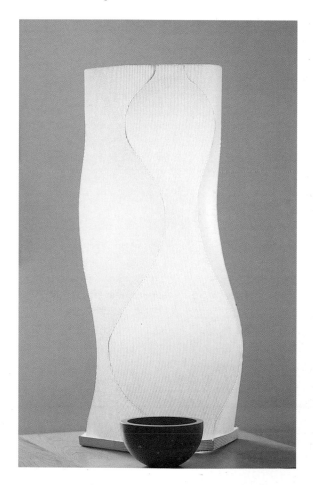

Light as design

While we seek to set practical light out of obvious sight, or use sleek fittings with simple shapes that pass almost unnoticed, with decorative lighting, we can afford to be a little more frivolous. This type of lighting is often utilized most during the evenings or for entertaining when a relaxed and tranquil setting is preferred.

The choice will be dictated by the particular space and the mood desired for that area. Over a dining table, a single pendant light that can be raised or pulled down when needed urges the light downwards drawing everyone into the conversation. Table lamps are more suitable for living rooms, generating a sensual overall glow and a relaxed feel. Choose simple shapes and set them in isolation. Elsewhere, architectural features or stunning pictures can be highlighed with wall lights, and pieces of furniture can be lit from below with lights set into the floor, creating dramatic shadows. And don't forget candles. Their flickering dancing light is enjoyable to watch and helps to create a mellow atmosphere in which to unwind.

As well as thinking about the quality of light created, it is also important to consider how the fitting itself will sit in the setting. Consider the form of the light and the shape of the shade. Look for arresting shapes, such as the sculptural form of a tall table or floor lamp that will throw a crisp silhouette against the backdrop of a wall. (See pages 76-77 for details.) A string of small square shades across a room can create a thread of delicate light which forms its own patterns, and can be hung or coiled to suit your purpose.

For shades and bases, look for natural materials such as a simple clay stand. Look out especially for exquisite handmade paper for lamp shades that reveal the exquisite quality of the fibers when the light passes through. Alternatively, make your own or adapt a shade you already have.

It is best to think about the practical and decorative aspects of lighting within a room as a whole, so that you can balance the different sources—the style of the light fittings and lamps, and their positions—at the outset to create a harmonious setting. A few lower wattage lights spread around an area are gentler on the eye—and soul—than one strong harsh light. You may need to experiment with the wattage and type of bulb in your lighting scheme to achieve the desired effect.

Remember, too, that the outside is important. Think how the view out into a garden can be dramatically changed by carefully placed outdoor light. Instead of looking out into a black hole, a subtle glow leads the eye onwards into the space, so that even in the confines of darkness our horizons seem open and infinite.

LEFT: The glow of candlelight brings a sense of peace and calm to any room.

75

Table lamp

The fine pattern of ribbed card formed into a curved silhouette creates a striking light source for any room.

YOU WILL NEED:

• **A1 sheet of ribbed white card (or similar stiff card)**
• **Piece of card for template**
• **White electrical tape**
• **Slim lamp stand**
• **Large knitting needle**
• **Scissors or Stanley knife**
• **Tracing paper**
• **Ruler**
• **Pencil**

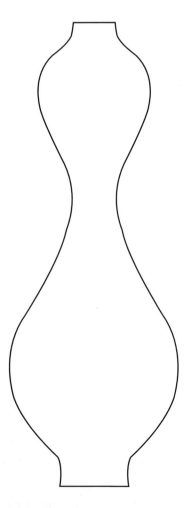

1 Cut a 2cm/³/₄in. strip along the length of the card (this will form the cuff at the base of the lamp). Enlarge the template to 23in/59cm. tall. Trace this onto the card and cut out the shape with a pair of sharp scissors.

2 Starting about 1cm/³/₄in. from the right hand edge of your piece of ribbed card, make three outlines of the template, each set about 18cm/7¹/₈in. apart at the base. Position the template a fourth time, as before, but only draw around the right hand side. Cut out the card around the outlines at either end. Gently score the remaining outlines drawn on the card with a pair of scissors or a Stanley knife, taking care not to cut right through the card. Bend the card along these scored lines so that you are able to form the card into a cylinder.

3 Cut about 15 short strips of electrical tape and fix them to a firm surface so that they are easy to pick up. Using the knitting needle gently work a small hole about 3cm/1¹/₄in. from one of the shaped edges of the card and about 2cm/³/₄in. up from the base (this hole will be for the electrical cable of the lamp stand). Bend the card round so that the shaped edges meet; place the pre-cut pieces of tape across the seam on the inside working the entire length of the join to keep the edges in place.

4 Fold the 2cm/³/₄in. strip of card in half lengthways, wrong sides together. Wrap the cuff around the base of the lamp snipping one half of the cuff to the fold line at each corner; trim off any excess. Cut about 15 short strips of electrical tape as before. Placing the uncut section of cuff around the outside of the lamp so that the cut section sits underneath to form a small flat stand, line up the snipped sections with the corners of the base. Use the strips of tape positioned on the inside of the base to secure the cuff in place, overlapping the snipped sections at corners so that the cuff sits flat. Position the lamp stand inside lamp and thread the cord out through hole at the back. Attach the plug.

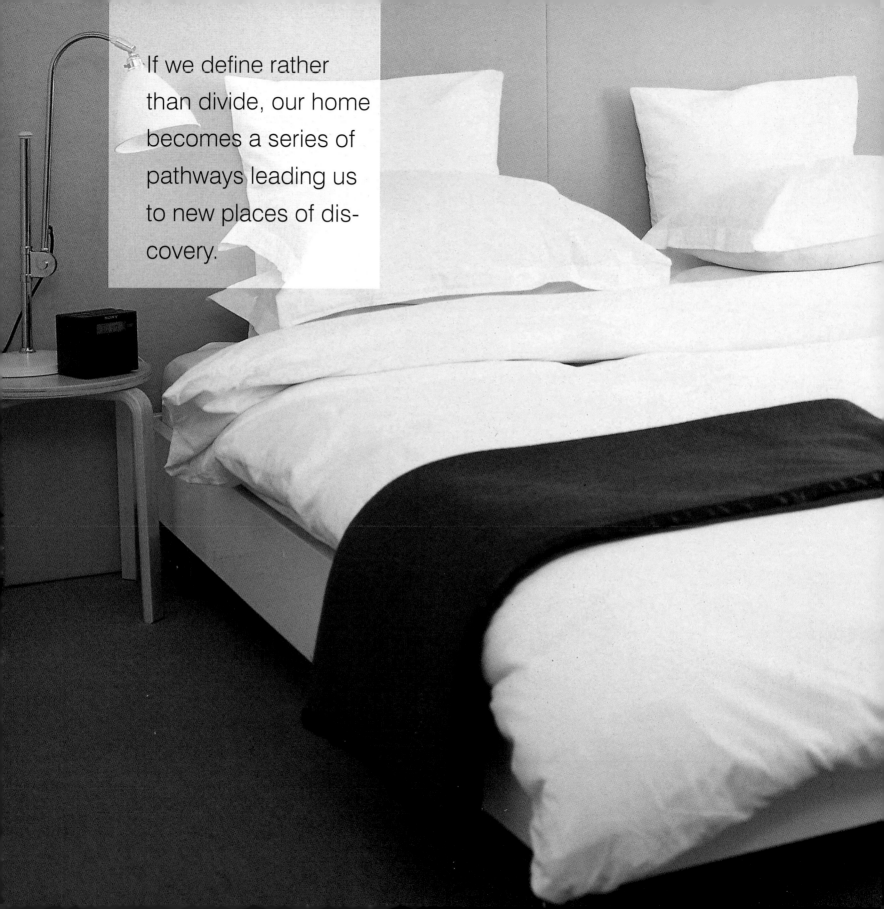

If we define rather than divide, our home becomes a series of pathways leading us to new places of discovery.

furniture
shaping the space

No matter how good our surrounding space feels, the true measure of success still comes down to the way in which we use it and are able to live within it. This is especially true of the Zen home, for if we are to find a sense of calm and balance here, we must first be able to feel comfortable as well as carry out day-to-day tasks efficiently and with enjoyment. The Zen home is not stark or clinical; It should not be an awkward place to live, nor one which requires us to adapt to it. Instead, it should fit us like a glove, existing snugly around us but without constricting us in any way. In short, it should feel like a home——a place to be used rather than just admired.

ABOVE AND BELOW: Wooden and wicker furniture provides an opportunity to add texture to our home and introduce natural elements.

The way in which we use a space is determined by the overall structure and how different areas connect with one another. However, it is the furniture that we place in these areas that defines how well the space functions. For this reason, our choice of furniture must always be a personal one, directed by an understanding of what we want from our home together with ideas about how we like to live. There is nothing worse, for example, than a kitchen that isn't planned with the way we like to cook in mind——cooking utensils on the other side of the room from the oven, or wall cupboards too high up for us to see into them properly. Instead of getting pleasure from preparing food we find ourselves constantly irritated and frustrated. Similarly, an uncompromising wooden chair might look sublime, but if impossible to sit on for any length of time, it will remain unused like a dead space and become cold and hard to look at. And there is little point contemplating the idea of high-backed armchairs, if what you really love is

a soft, enveloping sofa to sink into. Our goal might be simplicity and a streamlined look, but we cannot achieve this if our surroundings fail to nourish our soul.

OPPOSITE: A combination of wood and metal is used throughout this kitchen——from the units to the built-in table and the stools that emphasize a cohesive look.

Furniture decides the dynamics of a room. Whether a run of kitchen units, a bed, or chairs around a table, the shapes and arrangement of furniture breaks up the single space, creating new areas within it while retaining the sense of one open area. We can create different "rooms" within a single space by drawing on the furniture (rather than the structure) to define the different activities such as sitting, dining or working. For example, we achieve the sense of coziness and enclosure of a traditional living room by gathering a sofa and armchairs together in a group—when we sit there

we have a sense of being in a "room," while still remaining part of a larger space. The general result is a series of connected "rooms," separate but not divided. These pockets of space alter our view of a room, providing different angles from which to see our surroundings and so enriching our experience of the objects and elements within it.

In addition to providing us with the kind of contentment and organization that we desire, furniture must also find a level of harmony with the backdrop of the room as well as a sense of balance

The real voyage of discovery consists not in seeking new landscapes, but in having new eyes.

Marcel Proust

between the various pieces themselves. Just as with other elements in a home, we need to consider how to incorporate color, texture, form and decoration without detracting from the general openness of an area. Rather than thinking of furniture as a separate component, we should think of it as a device by which we extend the style and simplicity of our surroundings.

In keeping with the pared-down look of the Zen home, try to opt for less rather than more. Choose pieces for their purity of design, making sure the form reflects the function—whether for practical or relaxation purposes. If you find that there are pieces that you don't want, take them to your local charity shop, so that nothing is wasted.

RIGHT: In an open-plan arrangement, a table and chairs grouped at one end of the room create a natural dining area.

BELOW: Each piece of furniture can be enjoyed in isolation for the qualities it brings to a room. Here, a leather chair blends quietly with the other simple decorative aspects of the room.

Relaxation

Function

If the Zen home is about finding a sense of peace and calm, then comfort and relaxation are vital components for the feeling of well-being we experience there. If we cannot fully relax, then we cannot fully open our minds. The most streamlined of furniture can be the most relaxing as it allows us to focus on the experiential quality rather than the aesthetic—the comfort of the upholstery, the feel of the fabric, the way the shape of the piece molds around our body.

When we relax, we invariably want to lounge or lie down. The two items of furniture we turn to on these occasions are the sofa and the bed. While the sofa is a one-stop comfort zone where we can entertain and curl up when we are not at work, it is still our bed which is the prime place of relaxation, a place where we spend one third of our lives. We derive safety from the strength of the solid bed frame that is softened by the mattress, the inviting coolness of fresh bed linen and the all-enveloping warmth of a duvet or blanket, the combination of which enables us to unwind.

To truly relax, we need to be free of irritation, to simply sit or lie back and allow our senses to roam free. As a result, our sofa and bed should combine good support with softness. Mattresses that are not well sprung do not offer a good night's rest. Old sofas that have broken or damaged springs do not provide the requisite comfort to allow us to "switch off." Look for strong sturdy frames, good upholstery (that you may have to pay a bit extra for) and the healthy qualities of natural fibers in your choice of mattress, duvet, pillows and sofa cushions.

A well-planned layout is essential for efficiency in the Zen home. Aesthetics are important, but will count for nothing if the ergonomics of a room or area are not geared to our specific needs. The simplest decision, such as the height of a work station table and the relative position of a set of shelves above it, can be just as crucial as the entire planning of a kitchen or bathroom.

First, we must understand how we use a certain area and then devise a basic plan and layout on the basis of this. Try to consider even the smallest of tasks as well as the more obvious ones. We can also draw on the function of a room as the inspiration for the look. For example, why add unnecessary ornamentation to a kitchen to make it look more like a living area, when one could argue that it is function that gives the room its spirit, and that function should be accentuated rather than played down? There is something very striking about a streamlined kitchen of simple units and long empty work surfaces using displays of utensils and appliances as the decorative details. It conveys a sense of honesty, reveling in the function of the room rather than trying to disguise it.

Similarly, a strictly functional bathroom can have a sublime simplicity which focuses our attention on the element of water and cleansing—the elegant, sharp lines of a white ceramic bath or the symmetrical form of a plain, square basin and shiny taps. Rather than shying away from functional forms, we can embrace the purity of what they have to offer and in so doing, derive pleasure and enjoyment from the most ordinary aspects of everyday life.

OPPOSITE PAGE: A place that is easy to live in is more calming on the soul. This living area has low-level furniture, mixing a white sofa with warm woods and a shock of purple in the chaise longue.

Decorative

Old with new

Decoration is a rare but essential aspect of the Zen interior—indeed, Zen is a celebration of beautiful things. Introduce it sparingly through pieces of furniture placed thoughtfully into a simple setting for maximum effect. Set against plain forms, we notice the smallest of details, be they in the fine patterns of maple wood grain or the mark of an artisan.

The idea of decorative furniture doesn't just mean ornate—a piece of driftwood set on castors and transformed into a low table can bring its own decorative quality to a room. A plain white table dressed with a central well of shingle and some evocative shaped pebbles becomes a focal point at the heart of a sitting area—drawing us to the stones, which we can pick up and roll in the hand. (See pages 88-89 for details.)

The Zen home isn't tied to modernity necessarily, nor for that matter to traditionalism. It can be an eclectic environment that focuses on beauty, spirit, and quality rather than fashion, rarity, or value.

Old pieces add a sense of history and continuity to our homes whether, as family heirlooms, they have a historical connection to us, or simply that the evidence of time has left its mark on the surface. Classic designs of excellence from the past, such as a Mackintosh chair, seem to fit comfortably alongside more contemporary designs, linked by a common theme of purity and human spirit. In fact, the sharper images of modernity can provide a striking contrast to the less strident forms of older pieces.

But before you race out to buy more furniture, new or old, it is worth reassessing whether any items of furniture, currently in your possession, could be customized to meet your present needs. Pieces of furniture can be given a new look with paint: try adding a muted natural hue, such as sea blue or taupe, paint over with white or off-white when dry, sand away touches of paint to reveal the color underneath and create a gently-weathered appearance. A crackle glaze, applied between two coats of color, lends an all-over texture, similar in appearance to the rugged look of bark or the worn feel of peeling paint. All these treatments are good for adding character to new pieces of furniture or bringing color to older pieces that have lost their appeal. Using new fabrics to re-upholster old and worn pieces of furniture can add spice as well as change the emphasis of the piece.

BELOW: The majestic form of this gilded mirror is a stunning focal point in an all-white setting. The strong design is picked up in the decorative detail of the candle holders on the table.

Utilitarian

There is often a temptation to divide the furniture in our home: to put on show what we regard as part of a decorative scheme, and to disguise or even shut away the objects that we use rather than admire. Very few modern homes, for example, can exist without a television and stereo. One option is to lock them away. A better option is to choose compact designs that become simple blocks of interest in the simplicity of the setting—place them on the floor to create a strong shape contrasted against the wooden boards. And in many ways one could argue that such items are all part of the soul of a house – the music we choose to play, the program we switch on as an escape. Computers, too, have a similarly ubiquitous presence in homes these days. Instead of trying to deny their existence—by creating convoluted methods of storage, making them difficult to access—we can accentuate their modernity by setting them in isolation on a simple table, therefore, making them a part of the general theme of our home.

ABOVE: Utilitarian touches, such as the industrial appearance of this large chrome wheel can still be beautiful to look at, bringing a purity and honesty to our furniture.

LEFT: The rich mellow tones of aged wood lend a sense of history to the home.

Painted table

A simple painted table brings natural elements into the home by utilizing a decorative inset of stones.

YOU WILL NEED:

- **600mm/24in. square piece of 9mm/¹/₄in. medium density fiber board (MDF) or wood for the table top**
- **580mm/22⁷/₈in. piece of ply-wood for the table backing**
- **Four lengths, 25 x 65 x 650mm/1 x 2⁹/₁₆ x 26in. with each end cut down to a 65° angle for the legs**
- **500 x 17.5mm/20 x ⁵/₁₆in. dowel**
- **Jigsaw**
- **Primer and undercoat**
- **White eggshell for topcoat**
- **Polyurethane varnish**
- **Paintbrushes**
- **Eight 25mm/1in. screws**
- **Sixteen 5mm/⁴/₁₆in. screws**
- **Wood adhesive**
- **Drill and drill bits**
- **Sandpaper**
- **Bag of small stones**
- **Few pebbles**

1 To make the table top, mark a square in the center of the wood no larger than 30cm/12in. across (the table shown in the photograph uses a central square of 8.5cm/3³/₈in). To mark your square, draw two straight lines connecting diagonally opposite corners so that they cross in the center. Measure from this central point out along each diagonal to the required size of your square and connect up. Using a jig-saw, cut away the central square to leave a hole in the table top.

2 To make the legs: drill a 17.5mm/⁵/₁₆in. hole in the center of each leg piece. Slide the leg pieces onto the length of dowel, positioning two at either end in a cross to form the legs. Making sure the dowel sits flush with the surface of each outer leg, glue in place using wood adhesive.

3 With the plywood lying face down, position the legs and draw around them as a guide. Remove the legs and drill screw holes using the outlines as a guide. Turn the plywood over and place it on top of legs, and using the drill holes, fix into position using the 25mm/1in. screws.

4 Place the table base with legs attached upside down on the underside of the table top and screw together using four 5mm/⁴/₁₆in. screws along each side. Prime and under-coat the table, then sand down and fill where neces-sary. Paint the table with two coats of white eggshell and a coat of polyurethane varnish. Fill the recessed central square with the small stones and decorate the surface with a few pebbles.

The gaze that falls upon a single form comes to see that form completely. And in this way we see all that is around us with a fresh eye.

details an individual spirit

We bring our own sense of spirit to our home through the choices that we make. But it is in the details and the finishing touches that our true sense of self is fully expressed and our home becomes more of a personal space. No matter how wonderful a particular chair looks in a setting, for example, it still bears the presence of other people such as the designer and the manufacturer. We can transform it into something unique by the way in which we embellish it, the cushions we add, and the objects we place around it. The same is true of space itself – many houses have a similar lay-out and even when structural changes have been made, there is still a familiarity that can be seen elsewhere. Only when we add the final, individual touches, does it truly become our own space.

The most everyday items can embody potential for decorative touches. Things that we normally pass over should be looked at again with a keen eye, to see whether they can be used to create interest and detail in the new pared-back setting. As with other aspects, it is important to use details sparingly for maximum effect. We do not need to rush this process, as it is often best to spend some time in each room with the furnishings and decoration in place. This allows us to get to know each space more intimately and begin to have a sense of what we can use—what, if anything, we need to add and where. It may be that a touch of color is required, the furniture is too plain and needs some hint of texture, or perhaps a rug laid on the floor would help break up the simplicity a little. Adding details to a space is an ongoing process: until we introduce one element, we can not be sure whether others will be needed as well. Each piece should bring just the right accent and atmosphere to a space. And of course, just as our home is always evolving and changing, so might we change the touches we bring to it—brightly colored flowers might resonate perfectly in the sunshine of summer, but in the winter months, the more strident shape of a plant could be more appealing and appropriate.

Adding detail is also about adding personality. It is these irreplaceable touches, created by and for us, which truly make our home unique. A shell found on a memorable holiday, a picture painted by a friend, a home-made photo album, an old toy given to us in childhood. These are all the things which really bring soul into a home as well as making it aesthetically pleasurable.

OPPOSITE: A couple of delicate flowers in a small vase make the perfect simple detail.

The secret ingredient

Details provide the accent in a room. They shine out against the simplicity of the surroundings and change the rhythms of the room. As your eye roves around the room, it will come to stop at these small touches, carrying as much visual interest as a large wooden dresser or a bright colored sofa. A wall that seems too plain can suddenly be transformed by the addition of a picture with colors that harmonize with the rest of the room.

And we come to appreciate the quality of these accents when they are used in isolation—one single vase upon a shelf reveals more to the eye than a host of different shapes which merge together and become blurred and undefined. Similarly, a wall full of differently styled pictures and mixtures of different frames, presents a confused vision, one in which our experience of the pictures themselves is lost. Avoid the urge to over-decorate—arguably, we find greater connection with a single stone that encourages us to pick it up and hold it than with a pile of stones. When using details in the Zen home, the focus should always be on quality and not quantity.

The finishing touches

It is often by attending to the details normally overlooked that you can gain the most satisfaction. These are the finishing touches—the choice of light switch, the fine, discreet pattern of finger joints on the corner of a piece of furniture or the pewter vase on the dining table. These can sometimes be the hardest decisions to make. Door handles, for example, are one of the most common features to consider since they are used throughout the house and although small in size,

can have a tremendous visual impact. As with other things, we also need to think about what they feel like to touch and how easy they are to use. From a run of plain-fronted kitchen units comes the temptation to add embellishment, but simple touches that follow the clean lines of our surroundings can often have a more striking effect.

In some cases, decorative details may well be called for—a plain row of floor to ceiling cupboards can be given a spark of vitality with small, silver handles that catch the light. And yet, finishing touches don't need to be obvious—we can adapt stones to form door handles, or attach fine pieces of slate to light pulls or keys left permanently in doors as a decorative touch. Locks, especially for internal doors, are similarly important for the way they catch our attention, we might

We shape
clay into
a pot,
but it is the
emptiness
inside
that holds
whatever
we want.

Tao Te Ching

wish to invest in solid-looking traditional ones salvaged from an old house, thus bringing the past into our home.

Most of us already have the kind of objects around us with which to complete the look of our home. We do not necessarily need to spend money, but simply make a selective decision about what to have on display and what to store away. To keep the look serene and uncluttered, choose simple forms, elegant and understated but striking nonetheless. A stack of cream china or opaque glasses becomes a decorative highlight of shape and color when placed on display. A large cream bowl in the middle of a dining table is the only finishing touch that is required—every time we pass by we see the purity of the bowl's shape against the surrounding landscape and are reminded of its inherent beauty. Rows of storage jars in a neutral kitchen with different colored pasta, lentils or beans add welcome flashes of color and a row of utensils hanging from a bar lends subtle interest of shape.

We can be creative with the most ordinary of items—the use of brown bags decorated with photos from a recent holiday become a charming display, and a joyful discovery for visitors, when hung on a wall as a personal memento. An arrangement of woven baskets in a line upon the floor is an understated way of providing interesting texture—ordinarily we might disregard them as run of the mill, but set against a simple backdrop they form a striking visual decoration.

ABOVE: The curves of the bowl sit in contrast to the lines in the wooden table.

BELOW: A row of mugs mirrors the line of the shelf yet creates interest through repetition of shape.

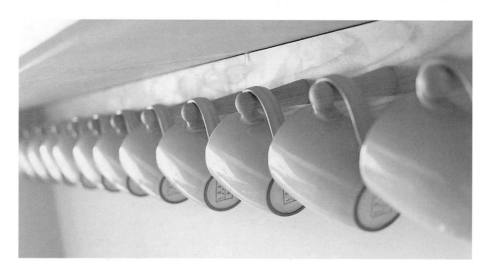

Warmth and softness

The hard edges created by clean lines can be blurred by soft and more pliant items, be they a casual throw over a sofa or rolled linen napkins on a rectangular table. Think how wonderful a pile of fluffy towels looks sitting against the straight lines of shelving. Cushions in particular are our allies in comfort, especially when covered in warm oranges, reds and yellows. Mix layers of more luxuriant fabrics together in moderation such as wool, cashmere, suede, mohair, velvet and corduroy to heighten tactile sensations.

LEFT: The smallest detail still has impact. Pure white serviettes rolled inside fine chrome rings add a classic note to a table setting.

LEFT: Look for ways to inject discreet pattern into soft furnishings, such as this two-tone knitted cushion cover with bobbles details.

OPPOSITE PAGE: Pile up luxurious layers with sheets, blankets and bed spreads.

Pictures

Pictures bring interesting blends of color to a room, and in uncluttered settings we are freer to add these colors as we like. Although framed pictures and photographs are the staple wall decoration in most homes, pictures should also be used sparingly for the colors to truly impact on our senses.

A large, single print or painting upon a wall can provide the cohesive element that brings a room to life, however, on a large expanse of wall, a row of similarly styled pictures with matching frames can reinforce the idea of sharp outlines and symmetry. The frame is just as important in its own right as the picture itself, so make sure that the image is not overpowered by the choice of frame. Take a look at nature for inspiration and ideas: bamboo, driftwood, oak, twigs from trees, shells, pebbles, and sand either forming the frame or embedded into it—the possibilities are endless. If something can be securely fixed to a base, then it has the potential to make an interesting and highly unique frame.

Experiment, too, with creating your own pictures. Place natural objects such as a row of pressed leaves or flowers into a frame. You could also match the picture to the frame.

Mirrors are an essential decorative element of any home, not just for practical reasons, but for the way they reflect light, open up the area, increasing the feeling of space. Choose mirrors whose frames match the interior design style and use them to open up dark corners or create extra length or width in a room.

LEFT: A panel of snapshots is given uniformity by using black and white prints only.

ABOVE: Pictures do not have to be set in frames. Here a picture is attached and hung on a brown paper bag.

Flowers and plants

There is nothing to compare to the luscious delight of a vase of flowers. The color, texture and smell bring life and vitality into our home and remind us of the overwhelming beauty of nature. In a room of neutral colors, the presence of rich blooms awakens the senses.

When you approach flower arranging, spend as much time considering the other elements of the art as on the displays themselves—the qualities of crystal clear water in a glass vase, unique markings on a handmade clay pot, a single stem seen in isolation in a tall vase or flower head floating in a large circular bowl. In keeping with the Zen style of introducing the outdoors into the home, think about creating a living arrangement. This can be done easily with a crop of mustard or cress on a plate, grasses in pots or herbs such as sage, rosemary, lemon verbena and basil in bowls. Line up a row of them in interesting pots for an unusual table decoration at a dinner party, or place them in the center of the kitchen table for you to admire as you use them (see pages 100-101 for details).

Plants can bring strong shapes and outlines to a room and offer a clean accent of simplicity. Think of architectural plants with spiky shaped leaves that resonate against other outlines in the space. Make creative displays with other vegetative matter, such as mosses with twigs and pussy willows.

RIGHT: A feast of floral texture and color along the window ledge is given visual uniformity by being set in similar brushed chrome vases.

Mustard and cress table decoration

Liven up a kitchen area or create an unusual centerpiece for a dining table with a crop of fresh growing herbs.

YOU WILL NEED:
- **Large packets of mustard seeds and cress seeds**
- **White cotton wool in a roll**
- **Large tray or plate**
- **Large plastic bag (to cover plate)**
- **String**
- **Shallow dish**

1 Cut five small oblongs from the cotton wool and wet thoroughly with cold water. Arrange the cotton wool on the tray and sprinkle alternately with mustard seeds and cress seeds, using a mixture of both for the central piece. The seeds should cover the cotton wool but not be laid too thickly.

2 Place the seed tray into the plastic bag and tie the end with string ensuring there is enough air inside to give the seeds space to grow. Place the tray in a dark, warm cupboard.

3 After about two or three days when the seedlings are an inch high, remove the tray from the plastic bag and place in a light warm room. Add a little water if the cotton wool looks dry.

4 After a few days when the seedlings have grown a little higher, place them in a decorative shallow dish to use as a table arrangement. Alternatively, cut the tops of the sprouts and rinse under cold water before serving.

If we can leave
behind all thoughts
and words our minds
can be open and free
and our senses truly
awakened.

sensual

elements for the soul

By and large we think of our home as a visual place, concerning ourselves mainly with the things we see: the forms of the spaces in it and the views it offers us. These factors provide the cornerstone of the quality of our surroundings and the atmosphere that is created there, but for a home to be truly sensual and create an environment that encourages greater relaxation, it needs to be able to stimulate all the senses, including smell, touch, taste and sound. Unfortunately, this element of home decoration is often left unexplored. The sensual touch is a less tangible aspect which we might find hard to express in words, but feel deeply nonetheless. It can be the smallest sensation, such as the smell of freshly ground coffee wafting through a room, or something more enveloping such as the sound and heat of a crackling open fire. Experiences that flow through us to which we respond intuitively without thought or words, arouse our senses in the simplest ways, releasing and clearing the mind.

BELOW: The aroma of ripe fruit stimulates the sense of smell and awakens the memory of how it tastes.

If we bring out the sensual side of our home, we add depth to the experience of living there. Fragrances can instill a sense of calm and invigorate every cell in our body. The sound of gently running water flows through us and induces feelings of contentment. The sensual side can even come from the things we do by acknowledging the importance of setting time aside to concentrate on ourselves. Moderation is the key. Light smells and sounds that delicately touch the senses rather than overpower them are better than those that are so strong they are all you can think about.

LEFT: Simple pleasures such as scenting bath water with herbs and bath salts encourage complete relaxation.

Scent

Small bowls of dried flowers or herbs can be used to imbue a bedroom with a light scent that enhances the sense of comfort. In a bathroom, a fresh, energizing aroma can reinforce our connection with the idea of cleansing and starting each day anew. Small stones or wooden shapes infused with fragrance provide a decorative textural display as well.

Aromatherapy is well recognized for its re-vitalizing properties. Essential oils can be used to promote well-being through massage and bathing. Lavender, for instance, is good for soothing anxiety and stress, bergamot is energizing, while geranium is uplifting, giving the spirits a boost. There are several ways that essential oils can be used around the house to release a subtle health-improving scent, particularly when placed near a gentle source of heat. Add a few drops of oil to a bowl of dried flowers or potpourri, padded clothes hangers or drawer liners, light bulbs, a specially designed oil burner, or a saucer of water placed above a radiator.

ABOVE: Use a line of bowls of dried flowers and herbs to decorate a windowsill or mantlepiece .

RIGHT: Essential oils have properties that are good for the body and mind. A collection of stones imbued with the a few drops of your favorite oil bring freshness to a bathroom.

There is no better tonic to our sense of smell than the presence of fresh herbs. Whether or not you have a garden, bring the outside in by growing a variety of herbs in pots or place them on a windowsill. They don't have to stay in the kitchen—a small rosemary plant by the side of a workplace, for example, can enhance memory and stimulate creativity through its aroma.

For nighttime relaxation, incense sticks or essential oil burners with a few drops of sandalwood or camomile used sparingly around the bedroom can induce a restful night's sleep.

TOP: Light a few incense sticks in the evening to help you unwind.

ABOVE: Look for blooms with a distict fragrance, such as a couple of glorious springtime hyacinths.

LEFT: An indoor lavender plant releases a soft aroma that goes almost unnoticed.

Water

Water is a key force of nature. In its presence, we are reminded of open landscapes and the smell and energy of the sea. It is one of the most sensual elements that we can harness in the Zen home, enlivening the senses of touch and hearing.

Water is possibly the ultimate symbol of purity, and in its presence we feel cleansed and refreshed, whether it is a glass of water or an invigorating shower. Water in the home, however, doesn't just have to fulfill a function, it can be aesthetic and calming as well. One way to do this is through decorative displays—a bowl of water and flower petals, floating candles, or a glass bowl of water and rocks is enough to remind us of nature as well as bringing color and texture into a room. Water is also about sound and movement—think of the rhythmic beating of waves against the shore, or the rushing rapids of a mountain stream. Listening and watching water has the same effect on us as flames crackling and leaping in a fireplace—both seem to hold us mesmerized. There is something inexplicably delightful about being able to hear the sound of water in our home. This can easily be achieved by placing a small water pump in a medium-sized bowl of water. Alternatively, you might wish to be more adventurous and make your own fountain drawing in other elements of nature as well (see pages 114-115 for details).

Water flowing over us, or hydrotherapy, is another way we can enjoy the magical qualities of water—the relief of stepping into a nice, hot bath after a hard day's work is an experience most of us relish.

ABOVE: Trails of moss are set against bamboo, water and stones to create a sensual indoor water garden.

RIGHT: The sound of water is one of the most relaxing elements you can introduce in the home.

OPPOSITE: It is easy to make a miniature water fountain. Just place a small pump in a bowl, cover it with pebbles and add water.

Pebbles on the riverbed, wavering: clear water. **Zen Haiku**

Ambience

Our home contains its own natural atmosphere and we further enhance this through the use of lighting, form and structure. At certain times we might wish to impose a stronger mood on a space in order to evoke a more dramatic atmosphere.

Candlelight is the most evocative way we can alter the ambience of a room. It is the most basic way of creating illumination, and yet it brings so many elements into play. There is the light itself, which, depending on the quantity or size of the candles, can be bright and glorious or dark and restful—perfect for moments when we just want to sit and do nothing. The flickering flame and the patterns it creates, provide an unfamiliar and ever-changing sight for the eyes—even the flame of the candle itself when alight, has a beautiful form of purity.

We can change these inherent qualities by repositioning the candles: set them in a cluster, spread them out along a shelf, set them high up or on the floor around a fireplace. If we place candles inside a lantern or a simple glass or vase, we can cast out a variety of different patterns and shadows into the room. Similarly, candles floating in water create an undulating sensation of light which can be used to form a soft centerpiece for a dining table or on an outdoor table on a still summer evening.

LEFT: Tea lights set around a bath allow you to forget about the rest of your surroundings and concentrate your thoughts solely on the pleasure of bathing.

RIGHT: Different ways of displaying candles can change the mood they set. Dark textural holders provide an earthy balance.

ABOVE: Nothing compares to the allure of a real log fire. It provides a grounding focus for any room, while the sound, smell, colors and heat refresh the senses.

RIGHT: Large candles with more than one wick make superb decoration in themselves. Place them on the floor and allow the silhouettes to speak for themselves.

ABOVE: Our pets are our allies when it comes to moments of reflection. When a cat is in the same room, we can be still and quiet and enjoy having another heartbeat in the room without feeling the need or desire to communicate.

RIGHT: Taking time to pamper ourselves is an important part of our daily or weekly rituals. Thinking only of ourselves for a short while reconnects us to our own needs and feelings.

Time for yourself

Humans are, by nature, social creatures and yet we still crave peace and solitude. Spending time alone with yourself is an important feature of reflection. But being alone is not the same as loneliness, for being alone on a regular basis can have positive effects—less stress, quality time doing what you enjoy the most, a chance to catch up with how you feel about your life. In Zen, this is known as "cultivating emptiness" and "doing nothing," both of which can help us to clear out the mind clutter.

Unfortunately, there is an attitude in society that people should be constantly busy, and we often feel guilty if we do not live up to this. However, "doing nothing" simply means that we keep all activity to a minimum while we reflect and recharge our batteries. In much the same way as spending time with your pets is a good "stress-buster," so too is spending time pursuing your own pastime. These moments of pleasure can provide the greatest source for contentment and relaxation. Make time to spend on things you like to do—hobbies, cooking, working in the garden.

We can also treat our spirit in ways that are not necessarily about doing something or pursuing a goal. It can be by simply being. Think about the sheer joy of breakfast in bed, or curling up on a sofa and enveloping youself in a woolen blanket while reading a thoroughly enjoyable book. Pleasure comes from pampering ourselves, taking the time out of our grueling schedules to make ourselves feel good—the luxuriance of bath preparations packaged in exquisite bottles or rose petals in a hot milk bath. Whatever it is that makes you really relax, is also the key to restoring balance between mind, body and soul.

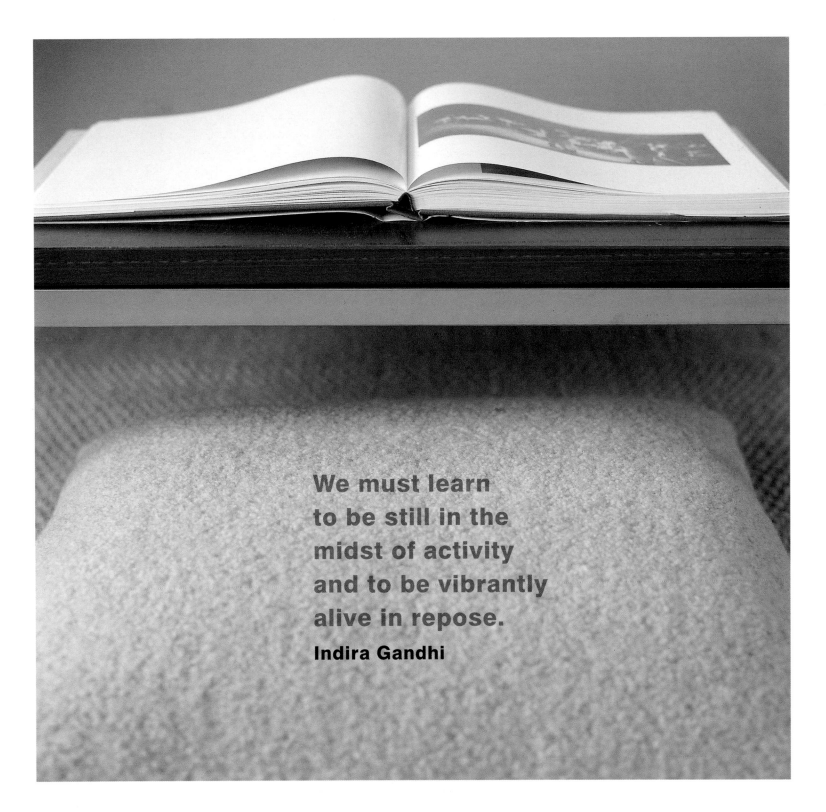

We must learn
to be still in the
midst of activity
and to be vibrantly
alive in repose.
Indira Gandhi

Water fountain

The sound of running water combined with the color and texture of natural elements, evokes the spirit of the great outdoors.

YOU WILL NEED:

• **Water feature pump, 450-liter/99-gallon capacity, maximum height 1m/3ft.3in.**
• **40cm/15³/₄in. of flexible hose to fit 12mm/¹/₂in. copper pipe and pump attachment**
• **Copper pipe, 600 x 12mm/25⁵/₈ x ¹/₂in.**
• **Large round dark plastic bowl, minimum diameter 36cm/14¹/₄in., approximate height 18cm/7¹/₈in.**
• **Galvanized wire 1mm/¹/₁₆in. thick**
• **25kg/55lb bag of large pebbles**
• **Drill and drill bits**
• **Hack saw**
• **Sandpaper and metal filler**
• **Exterior waterproof varnish**
• **Scissors and pencil**
• **Measuring tape**
• **Lengths of bamboo 15cm/6in., 7cm/2³/₄in, 5cm/2in and 1.5cm/⁵/₈in. in diameter cut to length (see instructions below)**

Note: The instructions refer to "chambers" in the length of bamboo; these are indicated on the outside of the bamboo by the circular grooves around the pole at various intervals along the length. When measurements for "chambers" are given, simply measure from these grooves along the outside of the bamboo.

1 To make the central section, cut a 64cm/25¹/₄in. length of 15cm/6in. diameter bamboo. You will need to adjust where you cut this section from the piece of bamboo to ensure the top has a 14cm/5¹/₂in. chamber and the bottom has a chamber of at least 6cm/2³/₈in. Using a 13mm/¹/₂in. drill bit, drill a hole down through the center of the chambers to take the copper pipe. Trim the pipe so that 10cm/4in. extends into the top chamber and 3cm/1¹/₄in. extends down into the bottom chamber. Place in position and use metal filler at the base of the top chamber to create a water-tight seal. Allow to dry. Using a 15mm/ ⁹/₁₆in. drill bit, drill a hole in the side of the bamboo 1cm/¹/₂in. up from the base. Push a little of the flexible hose through and fit onto the end of the copper pipe (the other end will be attached to the pump). Create a sloping top by trimming down to 2cm/³/₄in. lower at the outside edge

2 Cut the lengths of bamboo (measurements below) to form the ten pieces for the outer section, making sure that the top chambers are no longer than 20cm/7⁷/₈in. To help the water flow easily, cut the top of each piece at an angle so that they slope gently towards the outside edge.

7cm/2³/₄in. diameter pieces: 1 x 48cm/19in. 2 x 49cm/ 19¹/₃in.; 2 x 50.5cm/19³/₄in.; 1 x 53cm/20⁷/₈in.;

5cm/2in. diameter pieces: 1 x 53cm/20⁷/₈in.; 2 x 54cm/21¹/₄in.; 1 x 55cm/21⁵/₈in.

Measure 22cm/8³/₄in. up from the bottom of each piece (there should be a complete chamber on every piece above this line) and make a mark on each side. Drill a hole through these two points. Lay the pieces on the floor arranged in order of height with the shorter pieces in the center. Cut a 2.5m/ 8ft.1¹/₂in. length of galvanized wire and thread each piece onto it through the holes.

3 Mark a line around the top of the central section, 60.5cm/23⁷/₈in. from the bottom. Position the bamboo pieces on the wire around the central section and tie in place leaving a small opening at the back close to the exit for the flexible hose. Mark the center position of each pole along the horizontal line on the central bamboo piece, remove the outer section and drill a hole through each of these marks. To make the bamboo cuff for the bowl, measure the circumference of the plastic bowl and divide by 1.5cm/⁵/₈in. (to give you the number of short bamboo lengths you will need). Cut this number of pieces from the 1.5cm/⁵/₈in. diameter lengths of bamboo to the height of the bowl plus 2cm/³/₄in. Drill a hole near the top and bottom of each piece and then thread onto the galvanized wire as before.

4 Place the central section in the center of the bowl. Wrap the outer section around this ensuring the pieces line up underneath the holes drilled in the central section. Twist the ends of the wire together to fix the outer section in place. Wrap the cuff around the outside of the bowl and fix in place in the same way. Trim off any excess. Pull the flexible hose through the outer section and connect it to the pump. Place the pump in the bowl with the stones in the bottom to fix the fountain in place. Set the fountain in position and plug into the main supply, then fill the bowl with water. Switch on the pump—as the fountain fills up you will need to add more water (the pump should always be covered with water). Decorate the base with more stones. For a further decorative touch, set a couple of spare pieces of bamboo around the fountain and place a water plant and some moss inside.

Remove the debris that
clouds thought and vision,
and we shall find the truth
of our surroundings and
ourselves.

storage

uncluttering the mind

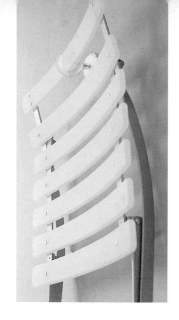

O ur mind becomes clear and open in a home that is free from the chaos of possessions. That does not mean living in a home without possessions, but in a place where all those items, so difficult to contain by virtue of using them are ordered and controlled or out of sight. It is not about hoarding or throwing everything away, it is about keeping a sense of yourself and your life's journey. Think how wonderful it would be to return each day to an environment such as this, and the atmosphere of calm one would find within it.

In some respects, a streamlined interior brings its own sense of orderliness, the discipline of straight lines and simple forms provides a cohesive frame that helps to tidy the view. But if we are to feel comfortable in our home, the Zen home must be able to cope with a certain amount of disorder. There is little joy to be had from living in a place where we must be obsessively tidy to preserve the general harmony. But too much clutter becomes oppressive, reduces the feeling of space and is a distraction from other sights and sensations in the home. If we want to keep the feeling of openness, then we need good storage systems.

Storage provides a compromise between the need for possessions and the need for space. It is about organization as well as tidiness so that we can accomplish tasks easily and without fuss. Efficient storage is not just about being able to clear things from view, but also about finding a way to streamline the appearance of objects and items—for in some cases, we may want to have things within reach, particularly in a kitchen or bathroom. Thinking about storage involves establishing systems for keeping the clutter level as low as possible, such as getting into the habit of recycling newspapers and magazines in regular

batches, rather than allowing them to collect into unwieldy piles. And, of course, we must also consider how to meld our storage systems with the theme of simplicity so that practical solutions become style solutions as well.

Successful storage needs to be well planned. Items that we need on a day-to-day basis must be close-at-hand and within easy reach; things that are rarely required can be stowed in less accessible places such as in the loft, cellar or garage. Try to divide your storage system into sections and organize the contents accordingly. Many shelves, for example, in a cupboard, give you plenty of space to store the contents making it easier to see what you've got—by comparison, two or three shelves piled high with items mean you have to sort through everything to find what you're after, and they are more likely to become untidy. Consider what needs to be stored and try and adapt the system accordingly. A wardrobe or area for clothes, for example, needs a variety of fittings—a rail for hanging shelves for your collections of sweaters and shoes, and perhaps a series of cubby holes in which to place small items or a run of pull out baskets so you can see what you're storing at a glance.

ABOVE: Storage can be as much about display as hiding things away. Here a folding chair is stored away from the floor space by a hook on the wall.

OPPOSITE: Simple storage ideas impose order on the most unruly possessions and keep surroundings uncluttered. A neat line of shoes offers decorative simplicity and provides visual balance to the long bookshelf above.

Out of sight

Storage units that seem to disappear into our surroundings,with possessions hidden completely from view, provide the most discreet solution. Cupboards are one of the most essential furniture items in our home because they can easily be adapted to the style of the surroundings, and they can be fitted with shelves or hanging rails, thus providing almost limitless options in terms of what you can store inside them. Cupboards that can be incorporated into the structure are the best, especially when finished with flat, plain doors and painted in the same color as the rest of the room so they can melt into the surroundings. Making changes to the structure of a room can provide a prime opportunity to create spaces for built-in cupboards. When this is not possible, look for dead space that can be converted without imposing on the openness of a room. Areas beneath stairways are perfect for cupboards. Alcoves, too, are good for both cupboards and sets of drawers, although in small rooms you need to make sure that they won't be too overbearing.

Consider encroaching a little on the space of a room by building a row of cupboards along one wall. They don't necessarily need to be very deep—a long hallway that ends in a blank wall can be adapted successfully in the same way. In some situations, cupboards can even serve to streamline irregularities—the line of an imposing box around pipes can be extended along a wall to form a cupboard, creating a stronger, more solid shape that looks as though it's meant to be there.

RIGHT: Deep drawers are ideal for storing bulky items such as sweaters and bedding.

Space beneath a bed is ideal for storage—it doesn't affect the atmosphere of a room and the space itself can not be used for anything else. Cupboards or drawers built into the bed frame extend the outlines of the piece of furniture itself. Where space (and room for storage) is at a premium, a bed set higher than normal can offer greater capacity for stowing things away. Alternatively, some form of a box on wheels which can be pulled out from under the bed also works well. Storage boxes mounted on castors are available in a wide range of styles and can be used in a variety of settings—at the side or beneath a work table, in a simple row against a wall, or even as an alternative to kitchen units, set beneath a work surface.

LEFT: Space beneath a bed is rarely noticed and often unused, yet makes an ideal place for an additional storage system.

BELOW: An alternative take on kitchen units, these wheel-out deep boxes are designed to fit beneath worksurfaces.

LEFT: The kitchen trolley is an essential piece of open-plan storage that can be stored away when not in use.

121

Dual purpose

RIGHT: A partition wall between a kitchen and a living area has been used as space for built-in shelves, so that videos can be stored close to the television, yet the sharp structual outline is retained.

BELOW: Positioning a headboard a little way from the wall creates space discreetly behind for storing clothes.

To retain as much space as possible we can look for storage solutions that combine more than one function. This helps to keep areas clear and simple, as well as lessen the demands storage makes on our home. A low chest of drawers, for example, might be used in a living room as a coffee table, a tall sturdy box or chest could also work well as seating (especially useful in small rooms such as bathrooms) or, if the right height, it could be utilized as a bedside table.

A panel behind a bed can be set a little distance from the wall to create a storage area behind—the panel functions as a headboard, while, at the same time, providing the frame for a cupboard system.

Shelving

No home can survive without shelving and, fortunately, their geometric form works particularly well in pared-down living spaces. They can be painted in the same color as the background for minimal impact or in a contrasting color to create a sharp accent. Alternatively, the color and pattern of natural materials, such as wood, can be used to introduce a streak of soft color in a pale space.

Consider how the shelving might be placed for structural effect as well as storage, and as a counterpoint to the vertical lines of an area. A large expanse of wall, for example, seems to be even longer when set with one elegant shelf that extends the entire length of the plane. Keep shelves as simple as possible to accentuate their

linear quality. Shelving in alcoves provides a set of clean, rigid lines which unify the objects stored there. Look for ways to incorporate additional shelving in unexpected places—a single shelf running beneath kitchen units, for example, provides slim, barely noticeable space for books and small items of crockery. We can also adapt the idea of shelving to other angular means of storage—a set of simple square boxes set in a row upon the wall can bring a sense of order to the mix of objects placed within (see pages 126-127 for details).

Simple displays on shelving provide striking contrast to the straight lines of their form—a curved silhouette of a vase, three simple elegant pictures in matching frames or a surge of color from a few flowers. Alternatively, we can use everyday objects to add color and texture—the spines of books, rows of vertically stored magazines, a run of identical glass storage jars colored by their contents. In keeping with the general Zen approach to the home, try to remove unnecessary objects by making thoughtful selections that form a striking visual impact against the surrounding.

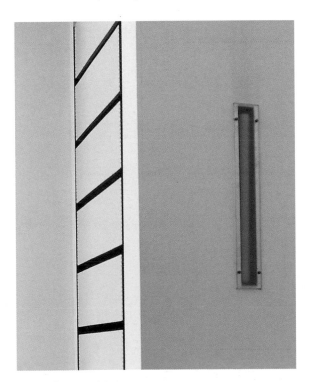

ABOVE: Shelves are the easiest way to give cohesive form to an eclectic mix of possessions.

LEFT: A tall stack of built-in drawers provides striking visual symmetry as well as a natural recess on the side, which could be used for a dressing table or further storage.

123

Storage as decoration

As with shelving, some storage systems can bring decorative qualities to a space. A chest of drawers, for example, with fine detailing or painted in a muted shade harmonizing with the pale color scheme, can become a simple focus in a room. Traditionally used in the bedroom, chests of drawers can work equally well in a hallway, as well as in a general living space. Unusual choices of furniture bring a personal touch too—a filing cabinet, sprayed white or ivory looks stunning in any space (not just a work area), old pieces, such as an antique wooden cupboard, which has a combination of drawers and shelves, can provide an interesting contrast to modern pieces in a room.

RIGHT: Storage facilities can look chic, as demonstrated by the sleek metal filing cabinets, and desk that can also stand as a shelf unit for displaying artifacts.

OPPOSITE LEFT: A modern take on a classic idea. The Shaker-style peg board enables you to display attractive utensils and kitchen essentials close at hand.

OPPOSITE RIGHT: The purity of white china and a collection of drinking glasses lend a simple decorative quality to a kitchen.

We can choose storage which allows the objects themselves to become decorative; we can show off the shapes and texture of crockery in a glass-fronted cupboard, framed by the outline of the doors. Large plastic-lidded bins which contain the chaotic shapes of different items allow subtle shades, shapes and texture to show through. Even ordinary magazine racks, in wood or clear plastic, bring regularity and shape to the objects stored there.

Look for more creative solutions which can be inexpensive to put together—a row of brown or white carrier bags on a shelf or set on the floor along a wall hide the objects stored within and create strong shapes (they can also be replaced easily when they become worn and crumpled). Similarly, a stack of storage boxes, in soft shades of gray, muted brown or pure white, become a strong decorative motif that reflects the symmetry of the structure.

Wall boxes

Strong lines and soft color provide streamlined regularity for household clutter.

YOU WILL NEED:

(for each box)

• **Four 100 x 230 x 15mm/3ft. 3in. pieces of wood or medium density fiberboard (MDF)**

• **Twelve 2cm/³/₄in. nails**

• **Hammer**

• **Sandpaper**

• **Woodfiller**

• **Primer and undercoat**

• **Colored eggshell for top coat**

• **Polyurethane varnish**

• **Paintbrushes**

• **Two picture hooks**

1 Place the short ends of the wooden pieces together to form a square box using three nails along each side to fix firmly in place.

2 Fill any holes with wood filler and sand the surface of the box to achieve a smooth finish.

3 Paint a coat of primer and a coat of undercoat on the inside and outside of the box. Allow the box to dry thoroughly between applications.

4 Apply two coats of colored eggshell. When dry, apply one coat of polyurethane varnish to protect the surface of the box. Fix picture hooks in place at either side along the top of the back of the box. Hang all three boxes by using a spirit level to mark a vertical line on the wall for positioning. Set the boxes about 10cm/4in. apart, hammer nails into the wall and hang the boxes in place.

Our life is frittered away by detail...
Simplify, simplify

Thoreau

Only through thought and contemplation can we find effortless liberation

putting the look together

defining your style

Achieving a sense of balance between the many elements that go into making our home a peaceful one is not something that happens by chance. A home that responds to the needs of the soul as well as the person, is one created from understanding those needs and finding ways to provide for them. We are all different, and we all have a different idea of what our ideal space for relaxing and living in should be like. And ultimately, the choices we make must be those that feel right for us and come instinctively from the heart.

Only by careful thought and consideration can we create a space that works well and is effortless to spend time in. When we think about planning our ideas, we need to take a holistic approach, considering all the elements of a space—the structure, the quality of light, how we use a room, the pervading atmosphere, furnishings and color—to ensure they work together cohesively. This is important whatever the scale of changes we are contemplating—altering the treatment of a window, for example, will cause a shift in balance in a room, so we need to be aware of all the different elements and how they will interact with one another to create a successful scheme. Our plan must also take into consideration the budget we have available and look for ways to adapt our ideas within this. Structural alterations are the most significant changes that we will make and need to be carefully throught out in consultation with a builder, or if the budget allows it, an architect, to ensure that they will not have a negative impact on the soundness of the building's overall structure. A plan also provides a benchmark to work from, which is a useful guide when making decisions, helping us to narrow down the options and giving us a feel for what will and won't work in a particular room or space.

That is not to say that our plan for a room should be set in stone. We need to be flexible and willing to adapt to "good" accidents or changes of heart that happen along the way. A home is something which evolves over time and we need to be prepared to work slowly, going back to the space in question as it takes shape and assessing how different aspects are working, adjusting our ideas to suit where necessary. An unusual item of furniture we come across and simply "must have," the discovery of a wonderful piece of fabric, a painting we fall in love with are all kinds of elements that can alter our notion of how we see a finished space. And indeed, it is these aspects that can't be planned ahead of time that give our home its unique stamp of originality.

Teachers open the door, but you must enter by yourself.
Chinese proverb

OPPOSITE: A balance between simplicity and pattern, color and neutrality, striking features and discreet detail has been achieved in this bedroom to create a clean look that retains a sense of warmth and coziness.

The basic structure

Creating a home that is liberating to be in is about balancing what you want with the actual structure of the building. For the shell of your home is the basic building block from which all other possibilities emerge. While it sets the scene for everything that is to follow and provides the potential for change, conversely, it also determines the extent to which change is possible. To be able to make the most of a space you must first understand its qualities—the way the light flows, how you move around in it and how different spaces may be linked together to create a more open, spacious surrounding. Removing walls to create an open-plan area may not be the only available solution. A large hallway running through the heart of the home, for example, may be the key to connecting spaces. By creating open doorways, or enlarging the openings, we link all the spaces together without losing the privacy of individual rooms. When thinking about the structure, you also need to address storage issues and consider where you will place your precious possessions.

If you are planning major structural changes, then you will probably require professional expertise and planning. Even here, you need to be clear about your own vision for the space—it is easy to get caught up in the excitement of someone else's stunning ideas without considering how they will really work for you. Always refer back to your own plan to make sure that your needs will be met by the new layout.

But you don't just need to think of structure in terms of major changes. You can breathe new life and freshness into a space in much simpler ways. Removing woodwork from walls, such as dado rails and wainscoating, can have a dramatic effect on streamlining the appearance of a space. Also think too about things you can change—perhaps there are built-in cupboards in alcoves which are too imposing for the space and replacing these with open shelving may help lighten up the area. Revealing the floorboards and painting them in a pale color helps increase the feeling of openness and space, while exchanging fussy window treatments for plain white blinds will accentuate the shape of the window and heighten its potential. Even the simple step of painting a room white can have a dramatic effect in terms of uncluttering the appearance of a room.

Inspiration

Very few ideas occur in isolation—we are influenced by everything around us and the images we see filter into our brain and are recalled, often without realizing, as a spark which then stimulates our own creativity. Inspiration can be found in all manner of objects and visual references. The accidental color combination of a flower against a backdrop, the colors in a holiday snap shot of a foreign landscape, the shapes and forms in a painting, a stranger's jacket, even the packaging of a particular product might be just the color you had in mind for your walls. If you collect all the visual sources together, you can begin to build up a picture of the kinds of shades, textures, patterns and combinations that you like.

Most of us find it hard to visualize how a scheme will look in the three dimensions of an actual room. Often, it's not until you see something that you can know if it will work. Interior design magazines and books are a valuable source of ideas for your home interior. Looking at how other homes have been put together can help clarify your own feelings about what you do and do not like, as well as suggesting ways in which you might adapt your own space, from color to structural solutions. They are also an excellent resource in terms of locating where to buy certain items. However, in looking at other people's homes you should also be wary. You need to view them as inspiration, let them lead you off down a particular avenue, rather than using them as a blueprint for your own living space. Lifting complete schemes is rarely successful, think instead of interpreting what you see and translating it into something that will be unique to your own home.

LEFT: Nature provides a wealth of inspiration. You can use it as a source for colors, patterns and textures, as well as using natural objects directly in the home.

Planning your ideas

OPPOSITE: Gather together pictures, magazine cuttings, fabrics, and paint swatches as a starting point for putting ideas together.

BELOW: It's a good idea to make a scaled-down plan of a room or space to help you look at how pieces of furniture will work within an area.

Having gathered an array of inspiring pictures, swatches and samples, you can begin to formulate a general vision of your interior space. Even if you are working on just one room it is worth considering the home as a whole—the impact of one room is changed by the atmosphere of another, the view that extends beyond, the color we leave behind.

Making a storyboard

Collect all the different swatches and scraps that you like and perhaps start a peg board to which you can clip them and start organizing a picture of your ideas. At the "inspiration stage" it is a good idea to be as open as possible and refrain from editing your selection until you come to put your plan together. It is also helpful to gather as many catalogues as possible to refer to when making decisions about the final scheme.

Drawing up a scaled plan of a room is always worth the effort—even more so in functional spaces such as kitchens and bathrooms. Make to-scale shapes of pieces of furniture you already have to see how they might be arranged in the space. As you work on your plan, keep going back to questions of how each space is used and what objects are needed to make it more efficient. You might also consider trying out particular areas by mocking up the layout to check that your plan really will work in the way you envisage—for example, is there enough space between a bed and a cupboard or will it be too cramped?

Also think too about the focus of a room—it may be structural, such as a large arched window, or defined by an area of color or an architectural feature such as a fireplace, and therefore other elements need to be kept simple so as not to compete with this. With fabric swatches at hand, you can also consider how different textures and patterns might be balanced in a room—lightness at the window, warmth and comfort for a sofa. Look for ways in which you can introduce simple decorative elements too.

force of nature

Artist Jonathan Cook's observations evolve into original, confronting images of the natural world and the animal kingdom.

Paints and materials

RIGHT: Different swatches of wallpaper and materials for a bedroom. By comparing and contrasting, you will be able to narrow down your selection until you find exactly the right combination.

No matter how accurate the paint charts, paint colors never seem to quite work in the way we expect. The amount of color in a room intensifies the shade, while different times of the day and the quality of light will also influence the finished look. The only safe way is to experiment. Use a length of lining paper (or the back of an old roll of wallpaper) the height of your room. Paint it in the color you are considering and then hang it in the room. Move the sample to different areas and at different times of day so you can really see how the color changes in the room. The paint type can also affect the quality of the color. Gloss finishes can be reflective and stand out in simple surroundings—if you want to accentuate the lines on the floor boards, gloss paint may be just what you need. On the other hand, matte paints such as emulsion for the walls and eggshell for woodwork, sit flat against a surface and are less distracting and imposing on the eye.

There is a growing choice nowadays in organic (natural) paints. The essential difference is that these are water-based, containing naturally occurring plant and vegetable oils, as opposed to non-organic oil-based paints that contain petrochemicals. Some manufacturer's are now producing water-based gloss and eggshell paints as well as emulsion, giving you the freedom to paint your whole room, from walls to woodwork, in natural paints.

Once you can see how the color is going to look, you can start comparing swatches of flooring and fabrics from your storyboard against it and making your final decision about these.

Natural materials are always a good choice for the Zen home, but natural does not always mean environmentally friendly. Although it is not possible to completely avoid all products with chemical sealants or finishes there are a few simple things we can do. Check that wood and wood alternatives such as bamboo and rattan come from managed sources, and try to use natural wood stains and varnishes such as shellac or linseed oil. When sourcing bed linen and cushion covers be aware of those with labels such as "easy care" and "non-iron," as these will have been treated in some way for the "benefit" of the consumer. Have a go at dyeing plain cottons and linens yourself with natural plant and vegetable dyes.

New life for old

Few of us are lucky enough to start every scheme from scratch and most of our ideas must also incorporate existing items into our plan. Part of planning our ideas is to consider how we can adapt items we cannot discard to fit into our overall vision. Kitchen units, for example, can have a style reinvention by painting each unit with a color that matches the surrounding scheme, and exchanging the handles for a more streamlined style. If the budget allows, you could also consider changing the door fronts, replacing them with plain pieces of wood or medium density fiber-board finished with paint.

We can treat wooden furniture in the same way—strip an old and faded piece back to the bare wood and paint it to bring out the grain or replenish the color of the wood itself, or use a coat of natural varnish such as shellac to gently enhance the grain. It might be possible to alter the appearance of furniture by removing some of the decorative detail or, again, changing door fronts or handles to spruce up the style.

Upholstered furniture can be given a new lease of life with different covers—inexpensive calico will work well against the pale backdrop of the Zen home, and as a practical consideration, can be machine washed if spillage occurs. Likewise, simple pieces of furniture, such as wooden chairs or canvas director chairs can be given a different look with a simple white loose cover. (See pages 138-139 for details).

LEFT: Cupboard doors can be given a quick facelift with eye-catching handles to bring them into your new design scheme.

Loose chair cover

Give simple chairs a new streamlined look with loose-fitting cotton covers. The following instructions can be adapted to fit any square chair with arms.

YOU WILL NEED:
- **Plain white cotton furnishing fabric 150cm/4ft. 8in. wide by length of your chair from floor at back to floor at front plus length of side panels (from top of arm to floor)**
- **Sewing kit and sewing machine**
- **Reel of white sewing thread**
- **Iron**

1 Take the following measurements from your chair (these will form the separate pieces for the cover) adding on 1cm/¹/₂in. all around for seams plus 3cm/1¹/₄in. at the lower edge for the hem. Measurements should be liberal (a couple of centimeters/inches bigger rather than smaller) so that the cover will slip easily over the chair.

2 Cut out pieces of fabric for the chair cover marking each piece clearly so you can identify which piece goes where. With wrong sides facing, pin the main pieces of the chair cover together—back, seat and inner side arm pieces—over the chair. Machine stitch along the seams, and press the seams open.

3 Place the stitched section of cover back over the chair, wrong side out and pin further sections in place. Remove and machine stitch in place and then press the seams open. Continue in this way until all the pieces for the cover have been joined together (check that the chair cover fits comfortably as you go; where necessary take a little more or less seam allowance). Remove the cover from chair. Turn the lower edge of cover over 1cm/¹/₂in. to the wrong side and press. Now hem the bottom of the chair cover to wrong side 3cm and pin in place—return cover to chair to check that hem is level. Machine stitch or hand stitch hem in place.

4 Trim the seam allowances and snip the seam turnings at the corners of the chair cover. Turn right side out and press.

A From floor at back, to base of back rest of seat x width of back
B Base of seat back, across seat and down front to floor x width of seat
C Inside arm panel, from seat to top of arm x length from back rest to front of arm
D Outer side panel, from floor to top of arm x length from back of chair to front
E Gusset for side of back rest, from top of back rest to arm x 4cm (plus seam allowance)
F Arm rest gusset, from top of arm at back rest to floor at front x 6cm (plus seam allowance)

photo credits

All project photography and the photographs on pages 1, 13 (bottom), 27 (bottom), 45, 57, 60-61, 63, 82, 94 (top left), 95 (top), 102-103, 106, 107 (top & right), 108, 112 (top), 133, 134, 135, were taken specially for the book by Peter Aprahamian.

Other photography reproduced by kind permission: *Livingetc* (listed by photographer): 44 Photography, 58 (left); Graham Atkins Hughes, 12, 25 (bottom left), 85, 97 (top right), 111 (top right); Peter Aprahamian, 16-17, 20 (bottom left & right), 21, 22, 23, 30-31, 34 (top & bottom right), 35 (bottom right), 37, 39 (left), 56, 58 (right), 69, 70 (bottom left), 71, 78-79, 86, 87 (right), 95 (bottom right), 98 (right), 123, 128-129, 137 (bottom & far right); David Barrett, 2-3, 27 (left), 81 (top & bottom), 93 (top right & bottom left), 120 (top & bottom); Craig Knowles, 119; Tom Leighton, 15, 26, 27 (top right), 47 (top), 62, 83 (bottom left), 92, 97 (bottom), 98 (left), 121, 125 (right), 130; Hannah Lewis, 14, 94 (bottom right), 104, 109, 112 (bottom right), 136; David Loftus, 4-5, 54-55, 96, 105; Neil Mersch, 48, 49, 59, 74 (right), 111 (bottom right), 113; Jonathan Pilkington, 11, 50 (bottom right), 73, 111 (left), 122 (bottom); Ed Reeve, 25 (top), 50 (top right), 51 (right), 72; Trevor Richards, 124; Thomas Stewart; 34 (bottom left), 42-43, 50 (left), 68, 90-91, 99, 110, 116-117; Pia Tryde, 9, 44, 46; Chris Tubbs, 13 (top), 18, 66-67, 75, 83 (right), 87, 118, 122 (top), 137 (top left); Verity Welstead, 25 (bottom right), 35 (top), 47 (bottom), 51 (left); Henry Wilson, 32; Polly Wreford, 38 (top & bottom), 39 (right), 125 (left); Mel Yates. p93 (bottom right).

Peter Aprahamian, pp6-7, 36, 70 (top), 80.

Matthew Priestman, p24 (photographer Peter Aprahamian).

Many thanks go to the following companies for supplying items used in the original photography of this book.

Anne Musso, 4 Great Western Studios, Great Western Rd, London, W9 (0171 266 1776 for stockists), for the hand thrown bottles and bowls, 10 & 41, and the hand thrown porcelain bowl, 61.

Burlington Slate, 01229 889 661 (for stockists).

Conran Collection, 12 Conduit Street, London, W1, for the wooden bowl, 57 (bottom left), small wooden bowl, 74 (left) & 77, and wicker box and cushion, 139.

Egg, 36 Kinnerton Street, London, SW1, for the silk shawl, 10, tall vases, 13 (bottom), silk cushions, 57 (bottom right), large round bowl, 95 (top), small bowls, 106 (top left), and felt slippers, 139.

Interiors Bis, 60 Sloane Ave, London SW3, for the white armchair and console table, 13, and console table, 41.

Purves & Purves, 80-81 Tottenham Court Road, London, W1, for the wicker chair, 63 (top), 65 & 82, wooden side table, 74 (left) & 77.

Also, a big thank you to Mette Johnson, picture editor at *Livingetc*, for her patience and help with picture research for this book.

project index

index

First published in the United States of America in 1999
by UNIVERSE PUBLISHING
A Division of Rizzoli International Publications, Inc.
300 Park Avenue South
New York, NY 10010

© 1999 Jane Tidbury

99 00 01 02 / 10 9 8 7 6 5 4 3 2 1

Printed in Italy

Library of Congress Catalog Card Number: 99-71284